INDIVIDUAL EDUCATION PLANS

SPEECH
AND
LA GUAGE

net Tod and

ke Blamires

 **David Fulton** Publishers

B.S.U.C. - LIBRARY

00301675

David Fulton Publishers
2 Park Square, Milton Park, Abingdon, Oxon OX14 4RN

270 Madison Avenue, New York, NY 10016

First published in Great Britain by David Fulton Publishers 1999
Transferred to digital printing

David Fulton Publishers is an imprint of the Taylor & Francis Group, an informa business

Copyright © Janet Tod and Mike Blamires 1999

Note: The right of Janet Tod and Mike Blamires to be identified as the authors of this work
has been asserted by them in accordance with the Copyright, Designs and Patents Act 1988

British Library Cataloguing in Publication Data
A catalogue record for this book is available from the British Library

ISBN 1–85346–522–4

All rights reserved. No part of this publication may be reproduced, stored in a retrieval
system or transmitted, in any form, or by any means, electronic, mechanical,
photocopying, recording or otherwise, without the prior permission of the publishers.

Typeset by Textype Typesetters, Cambridge

BATH SPA UNIVERSITY
NEWTON PARK LIBRARY
Class No.
QS 371.914 TOD
Phil Dutch   30/11/09
DISCARD

Contents

Acknowledgements

The book resulted from work undertaken as part of a research project commissioned by the DfEE and managed at the Special Needs Research and Development Centre of the Department of Education with Canterbury Christ Church University College.

The authors would like to express their thanks to teachers and officers in the following LEAs who contributed to the project. The views represented in this book are those of the authors and are not intended to represent the views or policies of any particular body or LEA.

East Sussex
Hampshire
Humberside
The Isle of Wight
Kent

The London Borough of Newham
The London Borough of Tower Hamlets
West Sussex
The Wirral

In particular, the team would like to acknowledge the contributions from:

Tom Brown, SENCO, Woodside School
Colin Hardy, SEN Advisory Teacher, The London Borough of Newham
Garry Hornby, University of Hull
Keith Humphreys, University of Northumbria
Kate Jacques, St Martin's College, Lancaster
Mike Kelly, SEN Advisory Teacher, The London Borough of Newham
Bonnie Mount, Secretary to the Special Needs Research and Development Centre
Miranda Preston, Chichester Institute of Education
Tanya Sealey, Clerical Support Assistant to the Project

Many of the ideas in this book have been developed by, and with, teachers who have recently attended our 'Speech and Language Difficulties' courses at Canterbury Christ Church College. We are indebted to them in moving practice forward for pupils with speech and language difficulties and for their commitment and creativity in designing and implementing strategies and procedures which support the continued development of IEPs.

Preface

This book attempts to put forward a case for IEPs as part of a school's 'inclusive and effective practice' for the diversity of its pupils in response to the requirements of the Code of Practice and proposals in the Green Paper, 'Excellence for All Children'.

We maintain that IEPs should be part of a whole-school response to special needs. We have tried to avoid hectoring schools into reluctant compliance with the *letter of the Code*.

We have tried to encourage schools to build upon their existing good practice and to respond to the underlying *principles of the Code*.

Positive developments in relation to SEN provision have been triggered by IEPs. There now need to be adjustments to the thinking and writing of IEPs so that the rigour, previously often lacking in SEN provision, can be retained, and a responsiveness developed such that the educational component of the IEP can emerge. This is essential if individual progress is to be enhanced and inclusion influenced by the monitoring of schools' collective IEPs.

The logical consequence of any such development would seem to be a reduction in the total number of IEPs and an emphasis on practical monitored support. Hopefully this book will support the development of 'post-Green Paper' IEPs which aim to save paper and promote the development of educational ecosystems which foster the mutual development of teachers and learners.

Janet Tod and Mike Blamires
Canterbury
July 1998

How to use this book

This book is intended to help schools to consider their existing practices so that they can then adjust and modify them if necessary. Ideas and procedures contained here have been developed with practitioners in many different settings. The guidance is based on observations of current practice, and recognises that schools will be at different stages of development and will have differing resources. The impending review of the Code of Practice will be an opportunity for schools to reassess the effectiveness of their procedures in meeting the special educational needs of their pupils. This guide is intended to support this process.

The format of the guidance reflects three key aspects of the development of IEP procedures. These are:

Principles

Some schools have aimed to respond to the underlying principles embodied in the Code of Practice (COP) rather than to comply exactly with the IEP procedures described in the Code. This has allowed schools to regard a national Code while at the same time developing procedures which are manageable given their particular circumstances. For example, the IEP procedure as described in the Code has proved to be particularly challenging for some secondary schools and for schools with a relatively high number of pupils at Stage 2 and beyond. Each section of this guidance thus contains a section concerned with Principles to be considered by a school in interpreting the Code.

School development via Institutional self-review (ISR)

Effective schools have responded to the demands of the COP in general and IEPs in particular by integrating procedures into their school development planning. This has changed the perception of the COP from that of a set of prescriptions with the emphasis on individual rights and responsibilities to a document which informs and guides an ongoing process of collaborative school development for effective SEN provision. Schools are increasingly recognising the need to encourage shared responsibility for IEP procedures and to harness the resources afforded by the collaboration of parents, pupils and outside agencies. Each section of this guidance contains an ISR to enable schools to self-assess and to develop their own action plans.

Ideas for action

Many schools have found that some class and subject teachers need to be supported in developing skills beyond planning IEPs' targets, to include strategies for their implementation, monitoring and evaluation. Some schools are developing their own shared strategy banks; others are using strategies contained in published SENCO support packs as a starting point. A development which is becoming more evident in schools is the increasing use of technology (e.g. the world wide web) for the sharing and exchange of strategies for meeting SEN. Each section of the guidance contains some Ideas for action for consideration.

The section headings reflect the fact that the IEP procedure for schools is embedded within the development of assessment and monitoring procedures for all pupils. The sections on 'Assessment for target setting' and 'Monitoring' seek to illustrate how IEPs might be integrated into a school's general arrangements for assessing, and recording the progress of all pupils. The other sections have been included to address emergent areas of particular relevance to IEP procedures such as 'Using Information and Communications Technology'.

To use this guidance the reader simply has to view the grid on the contents page and select the focus of concern.

IEPs: Electronic communications

The SENCO Forum on the Internet has been the focus of professional discussion about IEPs and their utility and implementation. This book attempts to address the points raised by the following messages, which provide a flavour of recent debate (July 1998).

We SENCOs spent hours and hours trying to work out a catch-all format – in the end, whatever you do, you get the well-known cycle:

1. Target, method, who?, when?
2. Review.
3. Go to 1 again.

Paperwork gets repetitive unless methods are Named; but then parents (and some teachers) won't know what the named method is. I'm thinking of 'streamlining' this so that descriptions of all present Methods (from content to self-esteem via behaviour maybe) appear on a separate sheet, with recommended method highlighted, which is attached to the IEP so that parents get the picture (teachers too in some cases) as well. I expect everyone already does this...
it seems ages since IEPs were invented.
  The other sticking point is description of needs.

SENCO

My replies to my message about 'simple IEPs as per DfEE' seems to be – we looked at it and don't use it in our school because it is not suitable.
  Perhaps I am a bit naive here BUT if DfEE are saying this is a 'good' IEP are all of ours 'bad'?
  I am sure that Primary and Secondary IEPs will be different but do we need different versions per county and/or school?
  Is there not a 'committee' somewhere made up of ordinary/school based SENCOs, LEA learning support team members who could get together and devise a National IEP model?
  Could we not give some of our present IEPs to the committee and they could come up with an appropriate model?
  Am I missing something here?
  Perhaps we need to each send an IEP to David Blunkett or Estelle Morris.

SENCO
Mainstream KS2

Is there a need for IEPs in an inclusive curriculum? If we understand that term to mean a curriculum where the needs of all are addressed then either all students need an IEP or none. If this is so why are SENCOs barking up the IEP tree?

SENCO

In an ideal world, no and yes.
  IEPs are needed for those pupils who have a need which is distinctly different from everyone else in the teaching group. With a totally inclusive curriculum everyone's needs

would ideally be catered for and thus no one would need an IEP but is this likely to happen? If we all had lots of time, then everyone should have an IEP because everyone has individual needs.

Regards

SENCO

There cannot be a definitive reply since IEPs have taken on a life of their own within particular schools and/or LEAs. Any future guidance from the DfEE, however, is likely to suggest a simple rather than a complex version.

In truth, the original intention behind the Code of Practice IEP was not to get schools to write extensive detailed programmes covering either all the curriculum areas, or all of an individual pupil's SEN programme – the IEP (Code of Practice version) is a 'plan' *not* a 'programme' (as in the USA).

Good (or 'effective') IEPs are useful to all teachers who teach the pupil.

They were thought of as a summary of the main learning goals for the immediate future that all teachers should be aware of. Where there is a teaching implication to achieve these short term goals, IEPs can sometimes include these as well. In order to be manageable by the system and by all teachers, therefore, we are talking about half a dozen short term targets.

That will certainly be the advice that HMI will be giving to the DfEE following our third survey of the implementation of the Code of Practice.

Chris Marshall HMI
OFSTED

IEPs Ostriches or Meercats?

As contributors (but not final editors) of the SENCO red guide chapter on IEPs, we would like to offer the following contribution.

Because IEPs have been difficult to implement and maintain does not mean that they have not had benefits for children with SEN.

The emphasis on the paper tasks of the IEPs has sometimes detracted from the educational benefits of IEPs as a dynamic tool for planning, delivery and evaluation that helps schools become more effective in responding to diversity.

A SENCO and school need to know the incidence of SEN amongst the school's learners, what provision is being made to meet these needs and how effective it is.

Therefore some form of IEP is needed. Without such documentation it is difficult to involve other people on a long-term basis (staff–parents–outside agencies) in order to evaluate progress and adjust the approaches adopted.

Effective provision is about identifying SEN and harnessing available resources to meet those needs.

A plan helps when it sets priorities and roles which can be evaluated by all the stake holders in the plan.

We all like to think we are doing a good job but can we demonstrate that we are to ourselves and the other stakeholders in the IEP?

Who are the primary stakeholders in the IEP?

The learner, her parents, the SENCO (in a small school), the LSA or the class teacher?

Who are the secondary stakeholders?

OFSTED, the SENCO (in a larger school), the LEA, the Governors?

Ostriches and Meerkats?

Ostriches bury their heads in the sand and pretend everything is okay (allegedly).

Meerkats look out for each other (also allegedly).

Mike Blamires, Frances Castle, Janet Tod

What is an Individual Education Plan?

The term IEP refers to both a process and a document. The document serves two key purposes.

- *Education*: the IEP communicates the targets to be met and anticipated learning outcomes to all involved in its delivery. The document triggers action. For example, for a parent of a child with a language delay it might simply be a diary in which they record their child's response to ten minutes' daily additional input focused around a few targeted key subject words. This action, agreed with the SENCO, aims to support their child in developing understanding and usage of subject related topic words. By recording their child's response in a diary they monitor their part in the IEP and are able to provide summary information when it is reviewed. The same individual pupil would experience the class or subject teacher's action. Action might also be taken by a specialist from an outside agency such as a speech therapist. Each person involved in the delivery of the IEP is responsible for their own action and reports back summary information to the SENCO at times of review. Such a system reduces the detail that has to be written on the IEP. Action underpins the Individual Education Plan.

- *Accountability*: the IEP acts as a summary document which provides evidence and evaluates the additional provision that has been allocated to the individual pupil. The IEP document is thus central to in-school and LEA review meetings. Schools need also to review their IEP documents so that school effectiveness in relation to SEN can be evaluated and areas highlighted for school development, budgeting and resource allocation.

Why do pupils need an Individual Education Plan?

Clearly the function of IEPs is to allocate provision that is 'extra or different' to that at Stage 1. The IEP is not a compensatory device which makes up for lack of appropriate provision at Stage 1 but forms part of the positive action planning process central to the Code and should signal the need for additional educational effort.

The Advisory Centre for Education (ACE 1997) has noted that schools need to balance individual planning for pupils who have SEN with whole-school planning to secure good standards of literacy, numeracy and behaviour, particularly when the school has a suitable number of pupils who are underachieving and where many have SEN. Head teachers and the SENCOs should ensure that IEPs are effective, manageable and easily understood by parents, pupils and staff.

Individual needs may be considered to have arisen from factors within the individual, their family, the school curriculum, the school environment, their socio-economic environment or a combination of all these factors. The IEP procedure was developed in recognition of the fact that some pupils with SEN needed to have educational effort clearly focused towards meeting a few clearly defined targets irrespective of the complexities of attributed causation. *The IEP was designed to be additional to and not instead of other SEN provision provided by the school.*

What is an IEP?

An Individual Education Plan should set out:

- the nature of the child's learning difficulty

- action   – the special needs provision

           – staff involved, including the frequency of support

           – **at Stage 3:** external specialists involved, including frequency and timing

           – specific programmes/activities/ materials and equipment

- help from parents at home

- targets to be achieved in a given time

- monitoring and assessment arrangements

- review arrangements and date

(Code of Practice 2:93)

at the core of the Code's endorsement of the IEP lies a simple idea: 'if an institution or group of people gather their efforts round one or more straightforward objectives and review, after a specified time, whether these objectives have been achieved the desired change is more likely to take place'.

(SCAA 1995)

In the case of Stage 3 IEPs, this includes additional outside agencies. Figure 1 represents the different educational components of an IEP for a pupil with speech and language difficulties. The grid represents a concept of an IEP rather than a grid to be filled. Beneath the grid is the curriculum described in 'key skills' (English National Curriculum 'speaking and listening') to ensure that targets are curriculum linked. At the top are pupils' needs based on the idea of 'different or extra' (this is a relative concept depending on teacher expertise at Stage 1). These needs are translated into targets. The left hand side of the grid directs attention to the roles and responsibilities of all those involved in meeting the targets.

Many schools recognise that IEPs have been helpful in:
- providing a vehicle for the development of collaboration and involvement with parents, and a mechanism for enabling pupils to become more involved in their own learning plans;

- directing teacher attention towards the setting and resetting of clear, educationally relevant targets;

- involving staff in the development and implementation of strategies to meet those targets, thereby improving and sharing classroom practice;

- harnessing available resources to meet those strategies;

- increasing the emphasis on the *monitoring* of pupil *response* to teaching;

- providing clearer evidence as to the effectiveness of additional SEN provision.

How are schools developing their response to IEP procedures?

Schools and LEAs have made considerable efforts to comply with the IEP procedures described in the Code. However the pressure on SENCOs has been well documented and there is a clear need to develop systems and strategies to reduce this pressure while still adhering to the principles of provision embodied in the IEP procedures. The initial emphasis was on developing the IEP format, based presumably on the hope that if the paperwork could be solved then the process would follow. This has been gradually replaced by concerns for developing strategies which support the actual delivery, monitoring and evaluation of the IEP.

In many schools a large proportion of the SENCO's time is given to writing and reviewing IEPs often at the expense of enabling the SENCO to work with individual pupils. Some SENCOs, however have found that the training in the writing and reviewing of an IEP is a highly effective way of providing in-school SEN training for other teachers and support staff.

(OFSTED 1997, 6:68)

Concept of IEP for speech and language

Individual pupil needs

'English: speaking and listening' Opportunity for improving learning	Poor articulation	Inability to 'get out' what he/she wants to say	Lack of intonation, monotony of voice	Poor vocabulary, misusing words	Poor or confusing sentence structure	Using mainly simple sentence structure	Inability to follow verbal instructions, especially a sequence	Difficulty in learning common sequences, e.g. days of week	Tendency to forget names of common objects and people	Difficulty in learning to use clock/watch	Inability to recognise rhymes	Confusion of sounds in speech	Confusion of syllables in speech
Whole class													
Group													
Peer/pair													
CA/support													
Individual pupil													
Home/parent													
Specialist (i.e. speech and language t.)													
Outside agencies													

Key skills

Confidence
Building on their previous experience, pupils should be encouraged to speak with confidence.

Clarity
Distinguish between the essential and the less important, taking into account the needs of their listeners.

Coherence
Making themselves clear through organising what they say and choosing words with precision. They should be taught to incorporate relevant detail in explanations, descriptions and narrative.

Convention
Pupils should be taught conventions of discussion and conversation, e.g. taking turns in speaking, and how to structure their talk in ways that are coherent and understandable.

Cognition
They should use talk to develop their thinking and extend their ideas in the light of discussion. They should be encouraged to relate their contributions in a discussion to what has gone before, taking different views into account.

Concentration
Pupils should be encouraged to listen with growing attention and concentration, to respond appropriately and effectively to what they have heard, and to ask and answer questions that clarify their understanding and indicate thoughtfulness about the matter under discussion.

Communication
To communicate effectively, pupils should be taught the importance of language that is clear, fluent and interesting.

Figure 1

The Green Paper (DfEE 1997) raised questions about the lengths of some IEPs and the need for schools to tackle the growth in paperwork associated with IEPs. However, the need for adequate record keeping to monitor the effectiveness of SEN provision remains and IEPs are likely to stay on the SEN agenda.

Individual Education Plans: overview

Since the inception of the Code of Practice in 1994 schools have responded to the challenge to produce IEPs which 'identify needs, set specific learning targets, and assist teachers in planning suitable programmes in order to meet these targets and the pupils' needs'(Code of Practice 1994, 2.119).

'The preparation and maintenance of IEPs is the area of greatest concern for the majority of schools' **(OFSTED 1997)**.

Will the Green Paper's concerns for raising standards, 'shifting emphasis from procedures to practical support' (p. 5) and increased inclusion serve to reduce the requirement for IEPs? Or will the proposed reduction in Statementing result in a return to paper driven, evidence based IEPs for some SEN pupils? Will target setting (OFSTED/ DfEE 1996; DfEE 1997a; SCAA 1997) result in schools concentrating their resources on pupils at Levels 1 and 3 for literacy and numeracy and increase the number of pupils who are deemed to need 'extra and different' provision for literacy and numeracy via specific IEPs?

While it is untimely to attempt to answer these questions there is little doubt that the implementation of IEPs has done much to enhance the status of SENCOs and promote whole-school involvement in planning teaching and learning for SEN pupils.

This book starts with the premise that IEPs will continue to have an important role to play in securing monitored extra provision for some SEN pupils. The writing and implementation of IEPs are not a discrete activity which is nearing completion but an ongoing developmental process for schools which seek to meet the requirements for inclusive education for SEN pupils. There is a consensus of opinion that further developments of IEP procedures need to be directed towards refining the paperwork, increasing the emphasis on how IEPs can best inform teacher planning and, most important of all, ensuring that IEPs have a measurable effect on pupil progress. It might be useful now for schools to reflect upon the progress they have made and consider to what extent their IEPs are 'explicit, embedded *and* Educational'.

Explicit IEPs?

'Schools need to give greater attention, not so much to the specific details of the IEP, but how it relates to teacher planning' (OFSTED 1997).

During the initial development of IEPs, schools and LEAs interpreted the 'accountability' function of IEPs as being central to any evaluation of a school's IEP procedures. As a consequence considerable time is still given to very detailed documentation, often in the form of detailed description of activities. In schools where IT is not used to support IEP writing, valuable time is given to making handwritten adjustments to IEPs which involve repetition of original detail. While initially some inspectors gave credit to such endeavour and detail it is now recognised that there is a need for a change of emphasis in the writing of IEPs:

> Schools are worried and confused over the way in which IEPs are used by inspectors and officers for the purposes of accountability. There is sometimes a feeling that they need to withstand legal scrutiny rather than be a practical basis for individualised planning.
>
> (OFSTED 1997)

So how might the amount of writing needed for IEP planning be reduced? Some schools have invested in software to support IEP writing and maintenance (*The SENCO Guide*, DfEE 1997c) while others have allocated additional clerical support.

One further way forward is for schools to direct attention towards the fundamental purpose of the IEP. The IEP (Plan) is a static written document which triggers action (the Process) from all those involved in meeting IEP targets. It might be useful for schools to think of IEPs as being made up of:

- a brief document which is placed on record as the IEP;

- a series of monitored actions informed from the IEP document, these are delivered and recorded by teachers, parents, pupils and specialists, etc;

- a record card (pupil IEP) which may be owned and carried around by the pupil to record action which has been taken. This 'record' may be written in the pupil's work book.

The IEP format should contain the smallest amount of information needed to trigger effective action.

A simple IEP that conforms to the Code of Practice at Stage 2 could be:

Nature of child's learning difficulties: social communication.

People involved (by name): class teacher, learning support assistant, mid-day supervisors, parent, pupil.

Strategies and programmes: via agreed Monitored Action Plans for all personnel.

Targets:

- will read and follow his 'social story' (attached to this IEP) for eating at lunchtimes;

- will demonstrate that *he is able* increasingly to follow and monitor his visual daily school timetable;

- will demonstrate that *he is able* increasingly to play a structured turn-taking game with a peer or sibling while being supervised in a structured setting.

Monitoring: daily and weekly (to set sub-targets in relation to 'increasingly') (these may vary).

Review date: termly.

In this case all concerned have agreed what they are going to do to achieve the targets. This, and the child's response, will be recorded in the class teacher's planner, in the learning support assistant's monitoring diary, in the mid-day supervisor's log book, in a parental diary and in the pupil's exercise book or IEP record card. The amount of detail needed on the actual IEP document can be reduced if that detail is communicated via the MAPs (Monitored Action Plans) of those involved. For example, if in meeting one of the above targets the parent agrees to play a structured turn-taking game with her child and his/her sibling three times a week then that detail does not need to be written on the IEP. The parent takes responsibility for that part of the plan and reports only at regular intervals of review or when his/her MAP needs adjustment.

IEPs can also be reduced by evaluating them against Code of Practice Stages (see Figure 2).

Figure 2 seeks to illustrate how IEPs should not be regarded as compensatory devices which record details of the curriculum differentiation and small steps programmes which should characterise Stage 1 provision. They were designed to record the 'different and extra' needs of pupils in order that they can make progress in their learning. Thus if SENCOs examine their school's IEPs it is possible not only to describe the SEN population of that school but also to compute which 'targets' occur frequently. This enables a rethink of what 'different and extra' means within the context of their school. The aim for the SENCO should be to reduce the number of IEPs by reducing the need for 'different and extra' provision. Although there has been a perverse incentive for IEPs to be used to secure additional resources, OFSTED (1997) reports that *'often the burden of maintaining IEPs is a major factor in the number of pupils placed on the SEN register at different stages'*. In looking at their school's IEP targets, SENCOs could seek to reduce the 'writing burden' of IEPs by asking the following.

1. Do the distribution and type of targets currently in place suggest that provision for individual pupils could be improved by the development of language teaching at whole-school level and Stage 1?
2. Do some Stage 2 pupils share similar targets and need 'individualised' and not 'individual' provision which could be delivered via Group Learning Plans (DfEE 1997, p. 34)? Circle time activities described in the Strategy section would be suitable for 'Group IEPs' provided the response was individually monitored.

Another strategy for reducing the amount of IEP writing is for the SENCO to implement an in-school training programme designed to promote the development of writing for a specific purpose. Writing for planning needs to be distinguished from writing for reporting. Maintenance writing needed for the implementation and monitoring of IEPs has to be evaluative, not descriptive, and should always be informative.

Educational IEPs?

While IEPs have provided a vehicle for the achievement of specific targets for SEN pupils there remain very real concerns about the 'educational' effectiveness of the procedure for the pupil concerned. One major concern regarding IEPs is that intrinsic to their design is a

The function of IEPs at Stages 2 and 3 of the Code of Practice

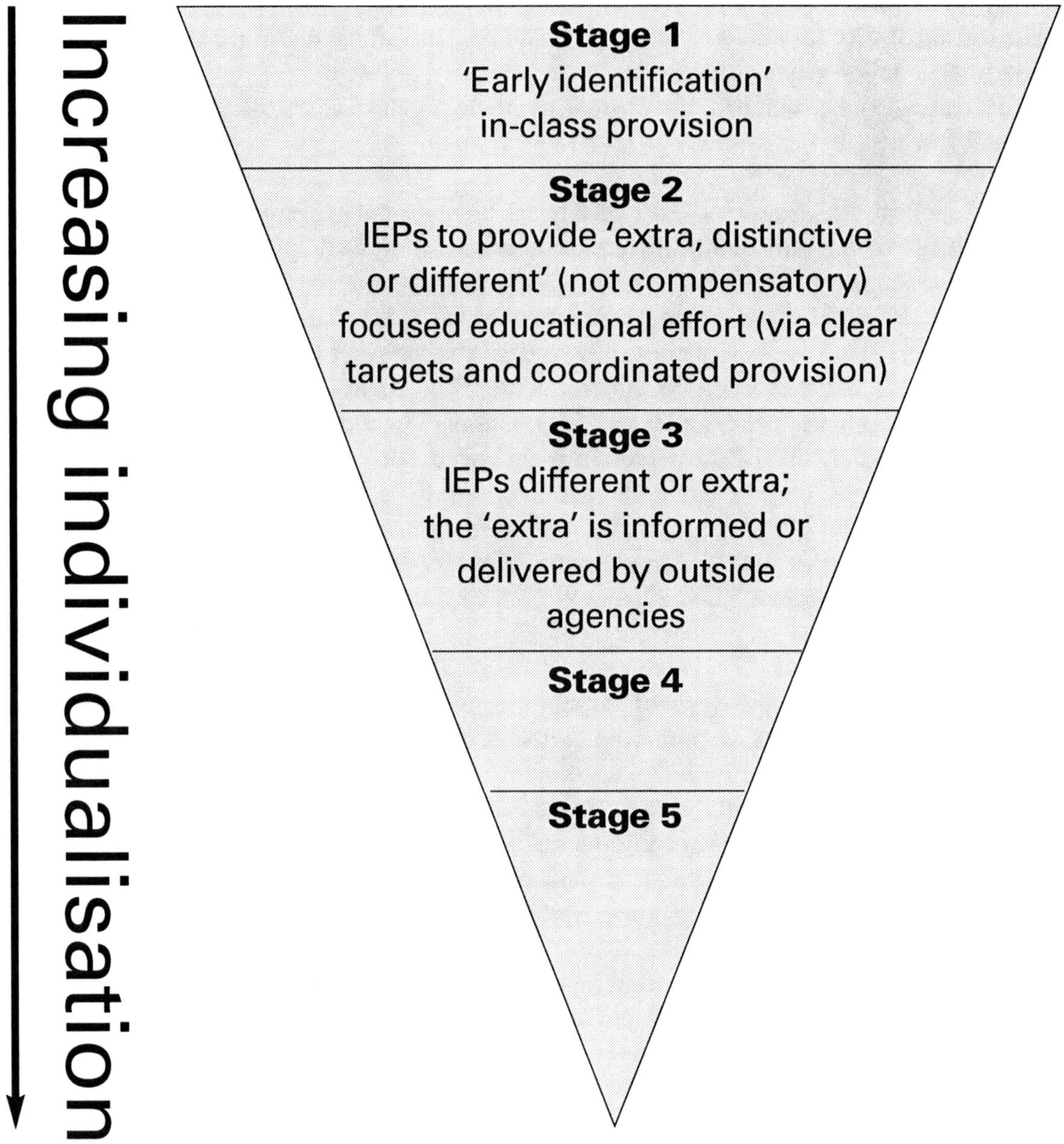

Increasing individualisation

Stage 1
'Early identification'
in-class provision

Stage 2
IEPs to provide 'extra, distinctive
or different' (not compensatory)
focused educational effort (via clear
targets and coordinated provision)

Stage 3
IEPs different or extra;
the 'extra' is informed or
delivered by outside
agencies

Stage 4

Stage 5

Figure 2

10

system of individual assessment, planning, monitoring and review which has proved to be too cumbersome to allow sufficient frequency of review for responsive adjustments to teaching (Hart 1988). This is of particular relevance for pupils with speech and language difficulties. In response to the Code's recommendations for IEPs it seems that concern for the curriculum and access across the curriculum has given way to a concern for the design and delivery of discrete packages of support whose impact can be readily and regularly monitored (Evans *et al.* 1996). Moreover, where the task is seen in terms of setting targets that are specific and measurable, the scope of 'support' tends to be reduced to a very limited area of a child's learning.

Hart maintains that *'providing additional support for an individual child should be part of the process of building an environment that supports the successful learning of all pupils'*.

IEPs in their inception clearly had a dual function, firstly to direct educational effort towards the achievement of a few identified targets with a view to bringing increased clarity and focus to SEN provision for the individual pupil, and secondly to enable the cost effectiveness of that provision to be evaluated. In practice, however, the accountability and resource allocation functions of IEPs have taken precedence over the educational function due to the need for schools to take note of how their SEN procedures are to be inspected.

As a consequence of the emphasis on procedures and accountability IEPs have developed with a heavy emphasis on written detail and SMART (specific, measurable, achievable, relevant and timely; Lloyd and Berthelot 1992). Support for the individual SEN pupil has thus been evidenced by compliant documentation and a restricted diet of targets, selected more for their assessability than for their relevance. This weighted interpretation and response to IEPs is the reason for concerns about their effectiveness. It is now timely to see whether the balance between compliance and accountability can be redressed towards pupil progress and educational relevance. The very fact that the IEP has a prescriptive set format is inconsistent with the notion that SEN pupils require support which varies according to individual need.

For example, the IEP format has to record the nature of a child's difficulties, which has encouraged a return to labelling, with IEPs classified as 'behavioural' or 'learning' and with planning and target setting frequently based on pupil 'deficits'. Targets are always allocated to the pupil even though for some pupils targets may need to be allocated to other individuals, in particular teachers or peers. The period review date carries with it the implicit assumption that this is appropriate for all those with an IEP and does not allow for the responsive and adaptive changes needed for those pupils whose responses may be very influenced by situational changes such as school or home factors. The emphasis on IEP procedural consistencies has thus tended to impose something of a strait-jacket on those involved in meeting the diverse needs and inconsistencies in learning and social behaviours that characterise many SEN pupils.

One way of improving the educational effectiveness of the IEP is to direct teacher training towards the principles of target setting and the role of targets in influencing pupil progress. Targets often prescribe 'more of the same' but in small steps with additional attention provided by LSA support. Whereas such targets can result in 'measurable' progress in the context in which they are met, it has yet to emerge whether IEP target achievement has a measurable effect on pupil progress across the curriculum and in the classroom setting (McNamara and Moreton 1995). 'Thus when designing and evaluating targets it is important to be aware that a successful IEP target should have an impact on pupil learning in the wider curriculum context and should be intrinsically linked to long and medium term planning' (OFSTED 1996).

Thus a narrow IEP target (taken from a speech and language IEP), such as 'will be able to use personal pronoun correctly', must be evaluated in respect of both the achievement of and the impact on the pupil's work in the classroom. A requirement that targets need to be assessed at two levels – achievement and impact – should address some of the educational concerns regarding IEPs. Similarly, it might be useful for teachers to consider 'who owns the target'. Should the target frequently seen on a language IEP – 'must listen and respond appropriately to teacher requests' – be written on an IEP or should such a target suggest to the teacher that 'instructions should be given in short clear units, having first secured the pupil's attention'? The ownership of targets is an important factor in the effectiveness of the IEP, particularly for pupils with language difficulties. Parental and pupil involvement in target setting is a powerful way of achieving 'relevance' and secures involvement in the process. **The notion of 'impact' on pupil learning and social behaviour may be used as a way of selecting which targets should be set for a pupil who exhibits a range of difficulties.**

Embedded IEPs?

'...the development of pupils' use of language should be integrated with teaching in all subjects' is the approach recommended by SCAA in *Use of Language: A Common Approach*. This document describes how the whole school should adopt an approach which encompasses the need for teachers to develop the following.

- *Knowledge:* concerning the role of language for learning and communicating.

- *Understanding:* of how teachers' work contributes to the development of communication skills.

- *Skills:* in structuring lessons appropriately in ways that support and stimulate language development; in identifying strengths and weaknesses in speaking and listening, reading and writing for all pupils, including those with SEN; and in 'monitoring and evaluating the impact of common goals and clear shared expectations of pupils' developing ability to talk, read and write effectively and, specifically establishing whether targets have been achieved' (p. 3).

The document views the development of the use of language as a whole-school responsibility with allocated roles and responsibilities (including the SENCO) and with a need for subject specific analysis in relation to language in which staff might:

- consider the aspects of language most vital in each subject;

- discuss the links between the aspects of communication required in the English orders and subject specific orders;

- identify how specific subject plans already include provision for language development and what new opportunities might be developed;

- identify longer-term objectives in each subject and how they can be built into schemes of work;

- consider how to build more opportunities to develop communication skills into classroom activities.

(Use of Language: A Common Approach, p. 4, SCAA 1997)

Guidance is also given in the document (p. 11) for planning for progression in both oral and written language. As an example, here is 'speaking and listening' progression across all key stages:

from:	to:
• simple answers to closed questions (one response expected)	• complex answers to open questions in which pupils explain their thinking
• discussion in pairs or small groups	• speaking to a larger audience
• listening to or giving a narrative account	• listening to or giving an analytical account
• listening to or using simple vocabulary	• using specialised vocabulary

Given that IEPs provide 'extra or different' provision at Stage 2 of the Code of Practice and beyond, it follows that the quality of provision for language development at whole-school level will influence the effectiveness of IEP provision. If assessment, target setting, evaluation and monitoring strategies are in place at whole-school level for the development of language then IEPs can be appropriately designed to provide *additional* provision for SEN pupils rather than act as *compensatory* devices. This requirement is particularly pertinent given the Green Paper's (DfEE 1997) change of emphasis for SEN pupils from 'integration' to 'inclusion'.

One of the key principles inherent in the design of IEPs is that response to the additional or extra provision IEP should be monitored so that effectiveness can be gauged. During the development of language in the natural setting, parents/carers provide directed, focused input designed to stress or 'teach' specific language skills to their infant, and then they seek to ensure that this new skill is practised and used in the richer context of reciprocal social communication.

Both adult and offspring monitor the effectiveness of communication and make appropriate adjustments, giving language use its characteristic flexibility. Thus while the IEP provides opportunities for focused 'teaching', so that essential skills can be developed, it is paramount that there is an opportunity within whole-school and teacher planning for the new skills to be practised, generalised and monitored. IEP planning provides specific targeted additional provision and at the same time needs to 'trigger' planning to ensure that the context in which the pupil concerned is expected to function has been appropriately modified – e.g. if an IEP target is concerned with the 'convention' aspect of National Curriculum 'speaking and listening' and the target set on the IEP is 'will initiate conventional start to conversation' then it is necessary for the class teacher concerned to know *under what conditions* the pupil is able to achieve this target and then to gradually move from the IEP conditions towards the 'normal' setting conditions of the classroom.

Initially the class teacher may have to 'cue' the use of the new response and peers would need to be encouraged to recognise it and respond appropriately so that the pupil is able to use his new skill in a variety of settings with the initial assurance that he will receive a positive response.

The requirement for assessment in context, monitoring the impact of the IEP, and the need to ensure that 'new' skills are practised prescribe that IEPs for pupils with speech and language difficulties are 'embedded' within the school and home context.

Very often demands emergent from central policy have created not only extra work but also a conflict of expectations. IEPs have created conflicts for SENCOs in that important specialist aspects of their job are being marginalised while paperwork takes priority. Proposed national standards for SENCOs (TTA 1998) recognises the complexity and importance of the SENCO's role and the inherent training implications. The Green Paper gives some hope for coherence of policy in relation to meeting individual needs, which hopefully will move IEP development forward in an agreed direction. However, once again SEN provision has been *integrated* (not *included*) into the White Paper's standards-raising movement. While mainstream pupils have been prescribed a Literacy Strategy (DfEE 1997), SEN pupils are allocated limited mention in the documentation, which alludes to the IEP as the vehicle for provision. No doubt another period of discovery learning for teachers and SENCOs will follow before attempts are made to address the conflicts for IEP development which are inherent in the Green Paper's subscription to the rhetoric on inclusion and the White Paper's prescription for targeted action for literacy and numeracy.

The IEP system had to be both rigorous and taken seriously at the outset if it was to be tested and tried as a mechanism for bringing increased efficiency and effectiveness to meeting individual needs. Positive developments in relation to SEN provision have been triggered by IEPs. There now need to be adjustments to the thinking and writing of IEPs so that the rigour, sometimes lacking in SEN provision, can be retained, and a responsiveness developed such that the educational component of the IEP can emerge and SEN pupils can be assured of their entitlement to additional, evidenced, monitored provision. This is essential if individual progress is to be enhanced and inclusion influenced by the monitoring of schools' collective IEPs such that 'schools continue to explore new ways of developing responses that value diversity' (Ballard 1995).

The logical consequence of any such development would seem to be a reduction in the total number of IEPs and an emphasis on practical monitored support. Clearly SENCOs have the key role to play in developing these 'green' IEPs, which aim to save paper and promote the development of educational ecosystems which foster the mutual development of teachers and learners.

Learning language is the solution – not the problem

Most children have not only 'learned to talk' but are also able to 'talk to learn' prior to school entry. For children who do not experience difficulties with speech, language and communication their ability to use language to communicate, reflect and reason, and plan and monitor their own behaviour, appears to happen with comparative ease. However, for those who teach pupils with language and communication difficulties progress is often frustratingly slow with little hope that the 'early identification' embodied in the Code of Practice (1994) and Green Paper (1997) will provide a solution to the pervasive effects language difficulties have on educational attainment. How do children learn to communicate and flexibly apply language with such apparent ease and at such a young age? Why do speech and language therapists undergo years of rigorous training when 'untrained' parents and/or carers can facilitate their children's language development in the home setting? Do teachers and learning support assistants (LSAs) need to know about normal language development if they are to effectively deliver an IEP for a pupil who experiences speech and language difficulties? A brief overview of some of the key factors in language development may be helpful in addressing these questions and contributing to planning for IEPs.

- Humans are born with the capacity to make use of symbols and code events, i.e. humans have a *'Language Instinct'* (Pinker 1994) which parents/carers activate and fuel during their child's early years. Even children reared in situations characterised by neglect and deprivation are able to communicate using language. The language instinct is powerful and appears to have an optimum time for activation – that is from birth to around three years of age, during which the infant develops from being a recipient of undifferentiated stimuli to becoming a social being who has mastered the attentional styles, language and reciprocity inherent in effective social communication. For children who have impaired language functioning the power and flexibility which characterise the release of the language instinct are much less evident and progress is considerably slower. Children who exhibit language delay and miss out on the critical period for language development (0–36 months) do not normally achieve the rate of progress observed in normal infants even when given additional language stimulation – possibly because the conditions which favour language development, i.e. individual adult attention and a considerable amount of conversation around daily caretaking events – eating, washing, etc. – are not available to the child as he/she becomes physically independent and more engaged in group and peer led activities.

- The initial impetus for the adult is to communicate with his/her infant by securing *joint attention*. This is achieved by closely monitoring the child's gaze and commenting on what he/she is doing. When the infant's gaze wanders to another focus the adult follows the infant's line of gaze and continues to comment. This enables two things to happen with time: joint attention to be secured and increased; and language and gesture to be received by the infant and associated with an activity or event which was initiated by the child.

- The *purpose* of language is *social* – the adult wants to relate to her infant and with time (6–9 months) the infant responds by wanting to communicate with the adult ('communicative intent'). A range of strategies are used by the adult to increasingly secure the joint attention and *turn-taking* needed for the development of social communication. These include: shared context – initiated by the child and extended by the adult; a considerable amount of commentary centred on repetitive routine events associated with the infant's dependency (i.e. feeding, dressing, etc.); active struggle and search for shared meaning, with the adult often giving meaning to the child's utterances; the adult *giving time* for the infant to respond and this response being valued by the adult. Child led activity and 'unconditional regard' lay the foundation for the development of self-esteem and in addition ensure that the child is successful in gaining adult attention. A child who is secure in their ability to gain attention does not usually continually seek it and indeed is more likely to cope with the parental separation experienced on entry to school and the need to share adult attention with the class group.

- During this period of development the adult uses STRATEGIES which follow the sequence: gain child's attention – modify input to ensure that it is relevant and understandable – extend and clarify using close monitoring of child's response and utterances to inform next sequence of language input. Strategies used include the following.

Gains the child's attention by:

- speaking in a higher than normal tone;

- whispering in the child's ear;

- using exaggerated intonation or rhythm;

- making use of the child's name to start a sentence;

- using special nicknames for the child;

- using eye-level contact, gesturing and pointing;

- showing, then hiding an object, so that the child 'waits' for it to reappear.

Reduces the complexity of input by:

- using shorter sentences;

- avoiding complex sentences;

- selecting vocabulary which is meaningful to the child, often using visual cues.

Extends and clarifies language by:

- monitoring whether the child is understanding; if not, speech is adjusted with key words being emphasised and repeated;

- speaking clearly and more slowly than in normal conversation, pausing between topics;

16

- the adult providing a commentary on the child's play, avoiding direct questioning;

- using 'here and now' familiar topics of conversation. If the child makes an error the adult does not correct but responds with the correct format: (Child: 'Look I writed my name'. Adult: 'You are clever to write your name').

So whilst it is important for teachers and LSAs to have a knowledge of the stages of 'normal' language development so that they can 'target' the next stage of development for their pupil it is probably even more helpful to reflect upon the 'how' of normal language development. It seems important to note that the basic impetus for language is a social one and that contexts make a difference. It follows that if teachers can 'set up' communicative contexts which encourage social communication then the pupil will be more motivated than if placed in a situation where he/she has to answer a question (to which the adult probably knows the answer). Arranging for the response to the curriculum to be framed in a 'communicative context' requires considered planning with emphasis on peer–peer, small group and collaborative groupings. In the adult–child setting often associated with IEP delivery it is important that the adult concerned (often the LSA) is trained to use strategies which have proved effective in naturalistic home settings, such as commentary on the child's activities, allowing time for the child to respond, securing joint attention, encouraging selective attention by the use of visual cues, etc., and which give opportunities for language to meet a personal and social developmental function as well being the medium for academic learning.

It is important to look at the purpose of language and the child's own awareness of the function of language. At home the adult uses language initially to make a relationship with her infant but once the child has developed language (around three years of age) parents skilfully change their communication style in order to prepare their child to use language 'to learn' in the school setting. Instead of merely communicating socially the adult adopts a 'teaching' style approach and asks the child questions to which the adult knows the answer ('What colour are your shoes?', 'How many plates do we need to put on the table?'). Similarly they move from seeking to establish 'joint attention' to developing in their child the skill of having their attention directed by an adult: 'Let's make a nice picture – find the red pencil and draw me a lovely apple'. They also try to get their child to sit down, listen and engage in school-type activities – reading, drawing, numbers, etc.

Parents can often offer the one-to-one attention needed for the initial development of this 'on task' behaviour. They encourage their child to make choices and to direct his/her own attention: 'What would you like to draw? Think about what colour you would like the roof to be. Can you be very clever and finish off the picture by yourself?' Feedback is often given so that the child can get used to being corrected and become aware of 'conventions' – 'Do you think the roof looks nice blue? – Houses don't have blue roofs do they? Why don't you colour it brown like our roof?'

Similar strategies are applied to enable their child to develop social skills needed for school. Their child is encouraged to play with same age peers and social behaviours such as listening, turn-taking, sharing, etc. are made explicit and rewarded: 'Here's some sweets – give one to Martyn and one to Peter – good boy for sharing'. These behaviours are developed in a supportive, safe setting for the child so that the chances of success are maximised. The important point to note is that these behaviours are explicitly taught and learned during the years prior to school entry. If a child does not have these experiences, and arrives in school without the appropriate 'learning behaviours', then he/she will find it difficult to self-direct attention, share attention with peers and use language for learning.

The purpose for which language is used in school is different to that for which it is used at home. Halliday (1975) reports that in the home context the purpose of language for the child is as follows:

Instrumental: 'I want'
Regulatory: 'Play with me'
Interactional: 'Shall we...?'
Personal: 'I love you...'
Heuristic (learning function): 'Why...?'
Imaginative: Pretend play...what if...?
Informative: 'I've got...'

However, once in school the purpose of language changes. 'Pupils' talking and writing provides evidence of their abilities to understand, imagine, explore, analyse, make explicit, evaluate, elaborate, interpret, hypothesis, and reflect' (SCAA 1997).

Children who experience speech and language delay prior to school entry may have difficulty in using language 'to learn' in the style and setting expected. It is important that this is recognised and that an assessment is made of any mismatch between the purpose of language used by the child and the purpose expected in the school setting, i.e. a child may exhibit a language usage bias, e.g. use language predominantly for seeking attention rather than for directing his/her own attention. It is the flexibility of content, form and use of language which enable it to be central to the development of learning and social behaviours required in the school setting. For most children this 'switch' of attentional and language styles to meet a purpose happens automatically. For others there is a need for a careful assessment of purpose and appropriateness in language usage so that changes needed are made explicit to the child and conventions are taught and learned in settings which have been designed to maximise the chances of the child achieving an agreed match.

In looking at how language develops in natural home settings it can be seen that the newborn is not regarded as having 'impaired speech and language functioning'. Rather the adult directs attention towards what the infant is doing and strives to use that as a context for experiencing shared meaning and developing reciprocal social communication. This is all-important and only when this is established does the adult seek to develop in her child the conventions, clarity, attentional styles and expressive language needed for 'learning'. *Clearly in the natural home setting language is the solution – not the problem.* There is much of value for IEP planning in studying the way in which children learn language naturally and the role adults and peers play in that process. However, in the school setting what is missing is one-to-one contact, close monitoring and adjustment, and the time for this 'extra and different' provision normally afforded the young infant. The IEP offers the opportunity to give such individualised targeted monitored provision and, provided that IEP planning is embedded within the curriculum and social activities of the whole school, then a balance can be achieved between the need for 'structure and emphasis' and the provision of opportunities for language use within a communicative context.

Language is the solution: Ideas for action

Key points for pupils with speech and language difficulties:

- encourage *active* processing, i.e. use discussion, review, appropriate questioning style, problem solving, reflection, etc.

- use *visual* strategies – cue cards, visual timetables, etc.

- make the *implicit – explicit*.

- give the pupil *time* to respond – if need be give the questions *before* the input to facilitate selective attention

- use *commentary* to encourage *joint attention*

- *assess* language in *context*, looking for consistencies and inconsistencies

- record and build on what the pupil *can do*

- think carefully about the *communicative* function of language when writing IEP targets, and their *impact* on pupil progress

- test *recognition* before *recall* (i.e. multi-choice before asking pupil to generate his/her own response)

- use discussion and visual planning to support the production of written work

OHP 2

'How can IEPs be integrated into the school's general arrangements for assessing and recording the progress of all pupils?' (OFSTED 1996).

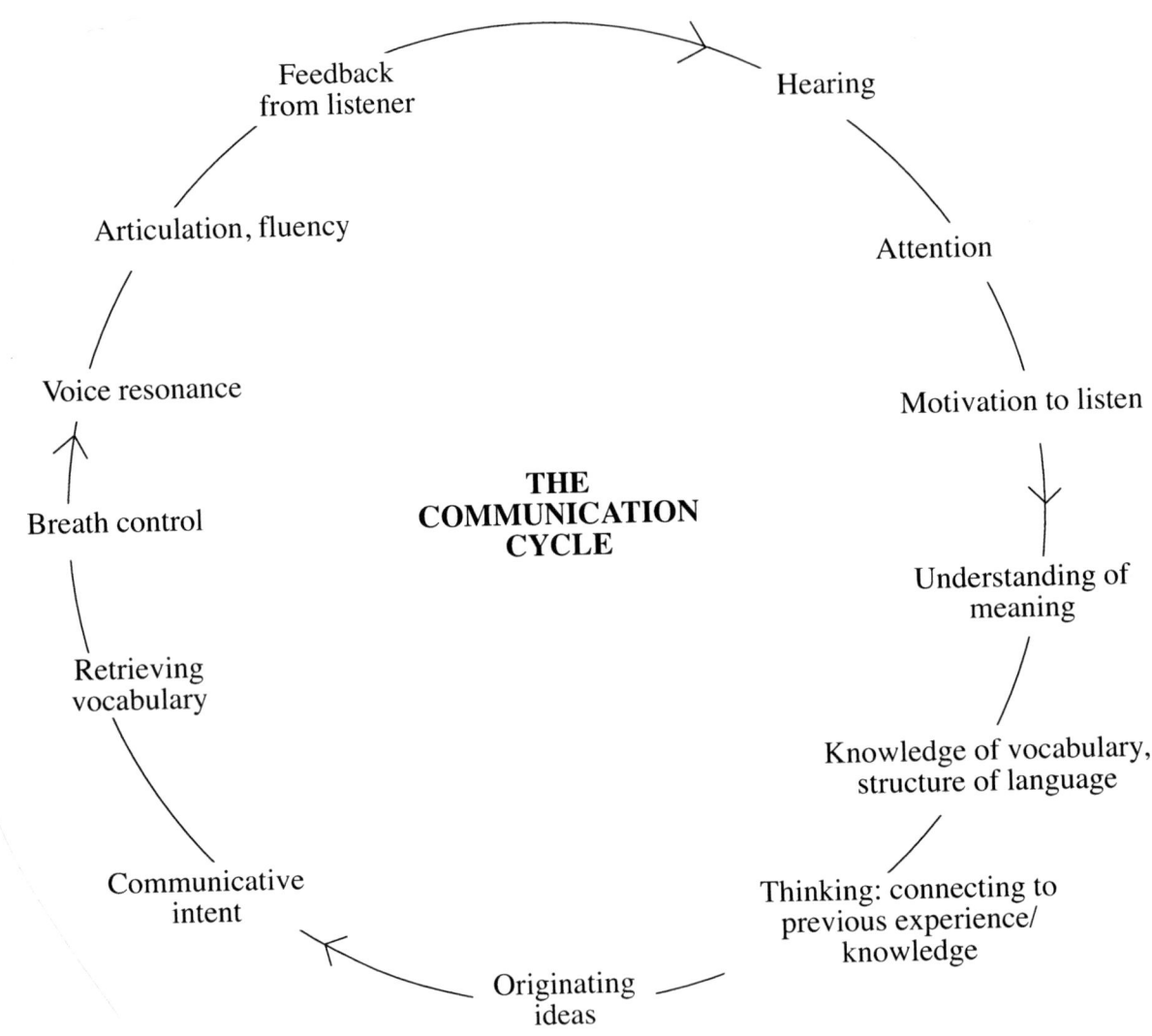

Assessment for IEP planning continues to remain challenging for schools owing mainly to both generic factors associated with whole-school assessment and specific factors which relate to the assessment of speech, language and communication – the complexities of which are illustrated by 'the communication cycle' (see diagram above).

As implied by OFSTED, there is a clear need to integrate IEP assessment arrangements into the school's 'general' arrangements for assessment and recording. Challenges for schools in this respect include the following.

- Agreeing a framework for the assessment of language and communication for all pupils so that individual pupil progress can be compared with that of their same-aged peers, with the result that an 'expression of concern' can be triggered and evidenced for assessment of pupil progress within the staged procedures described in the Code of Practice. It follows that any intervention including IEP provision should be delivered and assessed in the context of the medium- and long-term aims of the school's planning for language and communication. Figure 3 describes how assessment for IEP planning can be integrated into planning for curriculum delivery at whole-school level. The advantages inherent in inclusive IEP planning include a reduction in the paper-work and an increase in the effectiveness of monitoring.

- Communication of assessment information so that the recipient of the information receives more than a retrospective descriptive report. Collection and collation of assessment information needs to be *purposeful* to address the following questions.

1. What are the agreed areas of concern for this pupil?

2. Under what conditions does this pupil communicate/learn most effectively? This includes recording strengths and weaknesses.

3. What are the likely long-term aims for the pupil?

4. Which resources can be brought to bear to support pupil learning, (including human resources – parents, peers, etc.)?

If assessment information is interpreted, analysed ('What does this tell me about the way the pupil is processing information and how does this information inform IEP provision?') and reported in such a way as to inform planning, then time spent on assessing the pupil and collecting vast amounts of information which is then filed could be reduced. It may be that schools, as they move towards further development of their IEP provision, may consider examining the way they currently report assessment information to see if there might be changes that could be made so that assessment for 'extra and different' provision is made in relation to 'need' and not individual 'deficit'. For pupils experiencing speech and language difficulties it is not uncommon to see 'needs to increase vocabulary' targeted on an IEP. Assessment for such a target needs to take account of the school's approach to teaching and monitoring the acquisition of the language needed for subject specific learning and social communication (see: *Language: A Common Approach* (SCAA 1997) and to analyse the pupil's response to that teaching across a range of settings such that appropriate 'extra' provision can be designed.

Figure 3 links COP planning for Stage 1 and Stage 2 and 3 IEPs by using the framework for curriculum planning described by SCAA.

In addition to integrating assessment for IEP planning into the school's general arrangements for assessment, the assessment of speech, language and communication difficulties poses a particular problem in schools because of the following.

1. Language performance depends on the circumstances in which the language is elicited. Wells (1985) found that children's language varied according to the different contexts in which they were interacting.

2. Teachers often feel insufficiently qualified to assess speech and language difficulties. At Stage 3 and beyond of the Code it is suggested that external specialists' advice

22

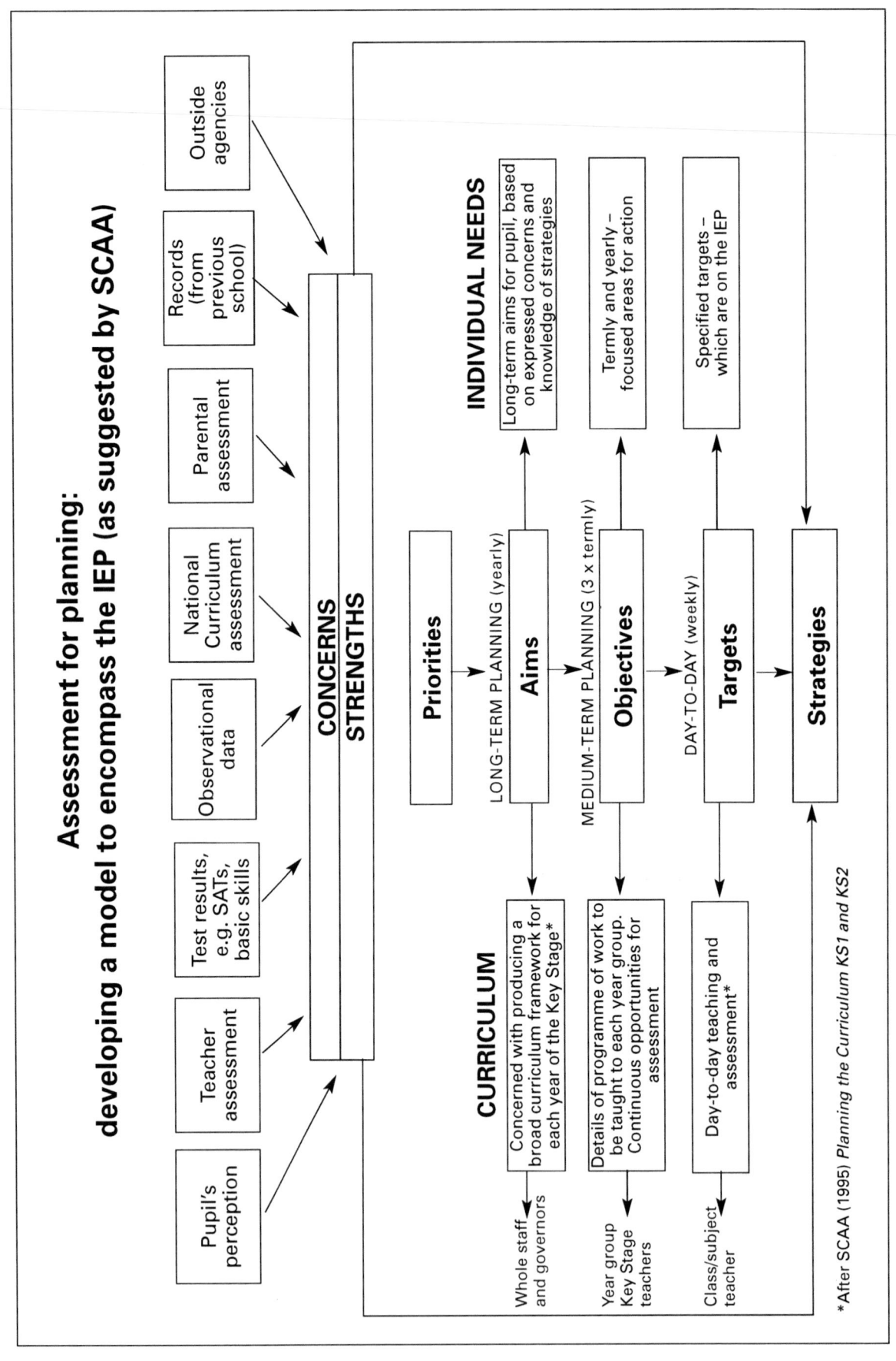

Assessment for planning:
developing a model to encompass the IEP (as suggested by SCAA)

Pupil's perception → | Teacher assessment → | Test results, e.g. SATs, basic skills → | Observational data → | National Curriculum assessment → | Parental assessment → | Records (from previous school) → | Outside agencies →

CONCERNS
STRENGTHS

INDIVIDUAL NEEDS

Priorities

LONG-TERM PLANNING (yearly)

Aims → Long-term aims for pupil, based on expressed concerns and knowledge of strategies

MEDIUM-TERM PLANNING (3 x termly)

Objectives → Termly and yearly – focused areas for action

DAY-TO-DAY (weekly)

Targets → Specified targets – which are on the IEP

Strategies

CURRICULUM

Concerned with producing a broad curriculum framework for each year of the Key Stage* — Whole staff and governors

Details of programme of work to be taught to each year group. Continuous opportunities for assessment — Year group Key Stage teachers

Day-to-day teaching and assessment* — Class/subject teacher

*After SCAA (1995) *Planning the Curriculum KS1 and KS2*

Figure 3

should be sought. In the case of pupils with speech and language difficulties the 'specialists' are usually speech and language therapists. In areas of the country where there is a shortage of speech therapy provision, teachers have been faced with the dilemma of deciding how best to meet the needs of pupils in their class who exhibit speech and language difficulties. This, coupled with increasing numbers of pupils with communication difficulties being placed in mainstream settings, and LSAs being given speech therapy programmes to 'deliver', has resulted in an increased demand by teachers for training in speech and language.

While there is no easy answer to the dilemmas faced by teachers in dealing with pupils with speech and language difficulties it is useful to note the following.

- Language and communication should underpin education. A study of normal language development describes how parents and/or carers facilitate language development in their offspring. Many of the strategies used in this context can be adopted by adults involved in teaching children with speech and language difficulties.

- Guidance written to support National Curriculum English 'speaking and listening' (*Language: A Common Approach* (SCAA 1997) contains ideas and approaches for teaching language).

Teachers frequently request information on how to 'test' children with speech and language difficulties and somehow feel that they need to acquire skills traditionally associated with speech therapists. It is useful to consider that teachers are skilled in the 'content', 'form' and 'use' model of curriculum delivery and assessment. This 'model' is used as a framework for assessment by speech and language therapists. For teachers it involves asking the following questions.

- What is the pupil saying (relevance, appropriateness, developmental level, etc.)? Is there a match between pupil 'content' and teacher 'content'? If not, what adjustments need to be made? Do such adjustments require the 'different or extra' provision prescribed by an IEP?

- How is the pupil using language? Is it in an appropriate grammatical form? Are available role models able to extend and develop grammatical format by example rather than correction?

- Why is the pupil using language? For what purpose is he/she talking and is there a match between this pupil purpose and what is needed in the classroom? Does the pupil monitor the effectiveness of his/her performance? Do those involved with the pupil hinder or assist his/her use of language?

Language is the medium through which teachers operate. They do so in a social setting. They manage pupils' language use in the school setting and have the same key role to play as parents/carers who manage the language development of children at home. Teachers have an important role to play in assessment and monitoring, and in setting up 'communicative contexts' for curriculum delivery and response. Further development and consolidation of teaching which fosters language development skills can best support the IEP process. The school setting does present particular challenges for target setting, which is not evident in the one-to-one closely monitored home setting of the physically dependent infant. These include:

- balancing the setting of clear achievable targets (focused teaching) with ensuring that achieved targets can be practised and integrated for social communication;

- working closely with those involved in the pupil's social communication network, i.e. peers and parents;

- designing and implementing monitoring procedures which recognise that effective use of language occurs within a time framed social setting;

- adhering to the requirement for '[shifting] the emphasis from procedures to practical support' (DfEE 1997a) while at the same time providing staff, particularly LSAs, with sufficient information to enable them to deliver and monitor strategies to meet IEP targets.

The next section seeks to provide information concerning the assessment of speech and language in particular and the use of 'frameworks' which support the embedding of IEP planning within existing curricular and assessment frameworks.

Teacher assessment

Teacher assessment which allows for observation on a daily basis is of immense importance. The 'one-off assessment procedures are of limited value unless they are considered together with information gathered on a daily basis' (Martin and Miller 1996).

Language should be assessed across a range of contexts. The core purpose of assessment for IEP planning is to enable the setting of relevant targets and the planning of appropriate provision for meeting those targets. The problem with the assessment of speech and language functioning is that contexts make a difference – that is, the performance of the pupil is influenced by:

- the learner themselves;

- the learning task;

- the learning environment.

For example, if *the pupil* has a social communication difficulty and has a problem with knowing what is required of the class group in any one particular situation he/she may become anxious and as a consequence may direct his/her attention away from the teacher and towards his/her own preferred activity.

The task may require comprehension and use of vocabulary which are too difficult for the pupil. The teacher may have prefaced the task with instructions which were too long and spoken too quickly for the pupil to have been able to hold them in sequence and retain them. Peers, other adults in the classroom and *the layout* might be such that the pupil is unable to selectively attend to relevant information. In this case the learning environment limits the performance of the pupil.

Under these circumstances the pupil would fail to respond appropriately to the task set and any assessment would record 'unable to...'.

Changes could have been made to any or all three of these factors, for example:

1. Learner anxiety could have been reduced by the pupil being given visual cues/explanation as to what was required of the class, and him, or perhaps he could have been allocated a peer 'buddy', LSA support, etc.

2. The teacher could have given out 'key word' sheets and discussed the vocabulary needed prior to giving the task, or differentiated the task to being one of 'recognition' responses (multi-choice) before giving the more difficult option of a recall task where the pupil had to generate his/her own response and put in correct sequence, etc.

3. The task instructions could have been given in short, clear sentences, preferably in a written format so that the pupil would have had time to process them and self-check whether he was doing what was required, etc. Under these conditions the pupil might have been able to respond appropriately and any assessment would have recorded: 'is able to...'.

Language is responsive and is influenced by antecedents and consequences. It follows that targets set for an individual pupil trigger 'targets' for those with whom the child is communicating (teachers, peers, parents, etc.). For example, some pupils who are assessed by classroom observation as having 'poor attention span' are criticised by their parents for being so engrossed in their computer games that they don't even stop for meals. In planning assessment for an IEP it is necessary to assess language functioning across a range of contexts. This includes across different lessons, structured and unstructured settings (lessons v. playground) and home/school, etc. For IEP planning at Stage 2 and beyond the pupil will have assessment data and records. A useful sorting activity involves the following questions.

- Is there any evidence of consistency in the observed/recorded language behaviour? As a guide if there is consistency across situations and between assessments from a range of people this tends to suggest that these are pupil or learner characteristics. These can be recorded on the IEP as 'strengths' and 'difficulties'.

- Are there inconsistencies across situations? What does this tell us? Under what conditions is language performance optimal, under what conditions is it minimal/impaired, etc.? This information is needed to provide teaching targets, setting conditions and strategies.

Finally there is a need to record what the pupil can do. This is important as in the natural language learning environment the parent/carer starts with the child's communicative response and then builds upon this so that it becomes extended and able to be used in a wider range of contexts. The aim is to place observed behaviour into a communicative framework with increasing independence starting with what is easiest for the child – usually 'adult–child-structured' as suggested by the setting in the context of social interaction.

The framework for social communication on p. 27 shows that important variables include:

- number of people involved in the communication;

- amount of adult intervention;

- type of activity: structured v. unstructured;

- amount of social interaction required;

- degree of autonomy needed.

Thus when target setting for pupils with speech, language and communication difficulties there is a need to describe the conditions under which the target is expected to be achieved. This is so that subsequent target setting makes reference to changing conditions and/or so that advice can be given to class teachers and parents as to how best to ensure that 'newly' acquired targets are gradually achieved in a range of conditions.

Staff involved in delivering and monitoring IEP targets may well benefit from receiving training in recording 'under what conditions' the targets are attempted. The school's IEP documents may need adapting to include a section to record 'settings' as described below. This suggestion does conflict with the aim of 'reducing paperwork' for IEP planning but if setting conditions are decided upon for any one school or subject area then these could be listed and ticked as appropriate. It is difficult to see how an IEP for a pupil with speech and language difficulties could have an impact on overall progress unless setting conditions are built into the planning procedure as described below.

Target: 'Will comply with instruction'
Setting:

Key points:

- observe and assess in a range of contexts;

- sort into 'consistencies and inconsistencies';

- tests are available – tend to test child in unnatural setting, time consuming, need specialist interpretation, etc.;

- record and work from what the child can do;

- record 'under what conditions';

- select targets so that they have an impact on pupil progress;

- record conditions under which target will be achieved.

	Alone	Parallel	Group	Interactive
Adult	Child may be colouring – adult initiated.	Adult sits next to child and colours her own picture.	Children are around a table all colouring/painting with adults.	Children are working together to produce a coloured picture/map for display with adult guidance.
Child/ pupil	Child is doing some maths in his workbook at a desk on his own.	Children are sitting around a table doing their own maths work.	A group of pupils are weighing sweets and putting them into marked packets.	Pupils complete a survey about pocket money and how it is spent so that they can produce descriptive data about their class/group spending habits.

Dependent ⟶ Independent

Structured	CA sits next to child and reads a book to him while he's playing in the sand	Child looks at book with adult	Child reads book to adult – told when to start and finish	Child reads silently in class when directed	Child selects a book from school library because he needs it for information to do homework	Child chooses a book and reads it for pleasure
Unstructured	Child plays with adult next to him	Child plays in playground with adult supervising	Child plays alone or watches TV unsupervised in house or classroom	Child plays next to other children with adult supervision	Child plays in small group without direct adult supervision	Child plays cooperatively with other children without direct supervision

Assessment for target setting: Ideas for action

It follows that if procedures for the Code should be integrated into the school's current assessment arrangements the first step is to see what assessment information the school already has which can be used to inform IEP planning.

In the nursery/primary phase schools will have in place baseline assessment and English National Curriculum 'speaking and listening'. In addition schools will be developing assessment schemes to support the implementation of the National Literacy Strategy.

Most schools will have regard to the principles which underpin the SCAA document (1997), *Language: A Common Approach*. It seems reasonable to use the information available to begin the process of assessment for IEP planning for pupils with speech and language difficulties.

In deciding upon a framework it is necessary to consider what assessment frameworks are currently in place within the whole-school system. Clearly central to SEN provision is the staged Code of Practice framework, which states the following under the section 'Speech and Language Difficulties'.

Code of Practice

i. There is a significant discrepancy between the child's attainment as measured by National Curriculum assessments and tests, and teacher's own recorded assessment of a child's classroom work, including any portfolio of a child's work and the attainment of the majority of children of his or her age.

ii. There is a significant discrepancy between the expectations of the child assessed by the child's teachers, parents and external specialists who have closely observed the child, supported as appropriate, by the results of standardised tests of cognitive ability, and the child's attainment as measured by National Curriculum assessments and tests.

iii. The child's expressive and/or receptive language development is significantly below that of the majority of children of his or her age as measured by standardised language assessment tests, or there is a major discrepancy between the child's expressive and receptive levels of functioning.

iv. There is clear substantiated evidence based on specific examples, that the child's communication difficulties impede the development of purposeful relationships with adults and/or fellow pupils and/or give rise to other emotional and behavioural difficulties.

v. There is any evidence of a hearing impairment which may coexist with, or cause, the speech and language difficulty.

(Code of Practice 3:86, p. 66)

Clearly the Code suggests that an examination of the pupil's response to the National Curriculum should be undertaken in order to identify between- and within-pupil differences in attainment. Normative tests of cognitive ability and language functioning are used to extend this information for IEP planning.

National Curriculum 'speaking and listening'

English National Curriculum orders (1995) laid down level descriptors for Key Stages and programmes of study under three headings, 'Key skills', 'Range of purpose' and 'Standard English and English study'. This is a relevant document for all teachers and in particular it provides the initial 'curriculum response' framework against which to assess whether a particular pupil who is experiencing difficulty will require SEN provision.

One useful initial framework to ensure curricular (i.e. English speaking and listening) relevance is to combine the Code of Practice staged approach with an assessment of key skills as set out in the English orders. This is described in the table below.

National Curriculum English 'speaking and listening' key skills*	Stage 1 of the Code of Practice: 'Does the pupil exhibit a discrepancy between his attainment and that of his peers?' (highlight plus supply evidence).	IEP planning: 'Are there discrepancies within the profile of the pupil?', e.g. highlight strengths and weaknesses.	Target setting: 1) 'What does this information tell me about the pupil's language processing?' 2) List and prioritise targets emergent from this assessment.
Confidence: Building on previous experience pupils should be encouraged to speak with confidence.			
Concentration: Pupils should be encouraged to listen with growing attention and concentration, to respond appropriately and effectively to what they have heard, and to ask and answer questions that clarify their understanding and indicate thoughtfulness about the matter under discussion.			
Convention: Pupils should be taught convention of discussion and conversation, e.g. taking turns in speaking, and how to			

National Curriculum English 'speaking and listening' key skills*	Stage 1 of the Code of Practice: 'Does the pupil exhibit a discrepancy between his attainment and that of his peers?' (highlight plus supply evidence).	IEP planning: 'Are there discrepancies within the profile of the pupil?', e.g. highlight strengths and weaknesses.	Target setting: 1) 'What does this information tell me about the pupil's language processing?' 2) List and prioritise targets emergent from this assessment.
structure their talk in ways that are coherent and understandable.			
Cognition: Pupils should use talk to develop their thinking and extend their ideas in the light of discussion. They should be encouraged to relate their contributions in a discussion to what has gone before, taking different views into account.			
Clarity: Distinguish between the essential and the less important, taking into account the needs of their listeners.			
Communication: To communicate effectively pupils should be taught the importance of language that is clear, fluent and interesting.			
Coherence: making themselves clear through organising what they say and choosing words with precision. Pupils should be taught to incorporate relevant detail in explanation, descriptions, and narrative.			

*Key skills from NC English speaking and listening have been arranged into 'C' word groups by the authors ('communication', 'coherence', etc.) to assist target setting.

Baseline assessment

From September 1998 it is a statutory requirement for all maintained primary schools in England to use an accredited baseline assessment scheme with all children starting in reception classes (or Year 1 if this is when a child starts school). Baseline assessment has two key purposes:

- to provide information to help teachers plan effectively to meet children's individual learning needs;

- to measure children's attainment, using one or more numerical outcomes which can be used in later value-added analysis of children's progress.

Prior to the introduction of baseline assessment schemes nursery and primary phase teachers had been given guidance concerning 'national' expectations via the document *Desirable Outcomes* (SCAA 1996). This describes expectations of progress and development within six areas: physical development, language and literacy, personal and social development, knowledge and understanding of the world, mathematics, and creative development. If the SCAA baseline assessment scale is viewed alongside these developmental descriptors it can be seen that the 32 item scale places particular emphasis on the assessment of progress in reading (12 items), and maths (8 items).

Speaking and listening are assessed via the following descriptors.

- Recounts events or experiences.

- Asks questions to find out information and listens to answers.

- Makes up own story and tells it.

- Makes up a story with detail and tells it to a small group, listens to stories.

Personal and social development are also assessed via a four item scale.

- Plays collaboratively.

- Is independent and keen to contribute.

- Concentrates without supervision for ten minutes.

- Expresses own opinions with a range of adults.

One of the promises inherent in baseline assessment is the early identification of pupils who are experiencing developmental delay or difficulty. While there are concerns that the use of an overall score as an indicator of developmental level may mask any particular speech and language difficulty it would seem important that schools make full use of the assessment information that they are required to collect. Although the baseline assessment is unlikely to provide 'diagnostic' information it should prove useful in addressing the following questions.

- Does this pupil score significantly lower than the rest of his peer group?

- Does this pupil exhibit any within-profile discrepancies?

- Does this information enable us to plan appropriate provision?

- Should further assessment be initiated?

One way of thinking about language which may provide a framework to extend information gained from baseline assessment for those pupils who appear to be developmentally delayed or impaired is to ask the following.

What is the child saying? *(content)*

How is he/she saying it? *(form)*

Why is he saying it? *(use)*

This format – *content*, *form* and *use* – is the model favoured during clinical assessment by a speech and language therapist as described below.

The development of language and communication: a framework for describing language

Language can be viewed in three dimensions:

CONTENT
FORM
USE

These components interact at different levels.

CONTENT	FORM	USE
Semantics: the meaning of words and how they relate to each other. Consists of *Vocabulary:* 'coat' *Concept:* e.g. colour *Categories:* e.g. food *Meaning:* 'I've spilt my milk on my blue coat'	How sounds are combined to form words (phonology) and words are combined to form sentences (syntax and morphology) – both according to rules. *Sounds:* 'p', 't', 'k' (phonetics), 'mat', 'hat' (phonology) *Words:* adjectives, verbs, -ing and -ed endings, plurals, etc. *Syntax:* phrases and sentences	*Pragmatics:* the reason why we use language to interact and the way in which we do it. *Why?:* intention *How:* did we go about conveying our message – did we monitor reaction of the listener and adjust accordingly?

(Bloom and Lacey 1998)

If a pupil does exhibit any delayed or inconsistent development in the areas of speaking and listening or personal and social development then it might be useful to carry out further assessment using a commercial package. Ann Locke (*Teaching Talking* (1985)) provides a comprehensive assessment and teaching package. Examples from this include a useful 'purpose of talk' for infant and junior age pupils against which pupil progress can be assessed:

Profile of language use: infant

1. Commenting and directing: child makes observations on people, objects and events; will direct others and assert self through talk.

2. Initiation of conversation with familiar adults and children: child initiates conversation with familiar adults and children by commenting or questioning.

3. Awareness of feelings: child is able to express own feelings appropriately, and anticipate and describe feelings that might be experienced by others in familiar emotive situations.

4. Awareness of social context: shows awareness of social context and modifies both language and speech according to situation and people present.

5. Use of questioning: child is able to initiate contact with others and obtain information about the present, past and future through questioning, e.g. 'What's s/he doing?', 'Where's s/he gone?', 'What happened...?', 'What will happen when/if...?'

6. Use of descriptive language: child is able to name and describe familiar objects/people using language of size, colour, shape, texture and function.

7. Reporting previous experience: child is interested in and capable of describing recent past events in approximate chronological order (with or without adult help, depending on age).

8. Reasoning/explaining: child is able to use language to reason: can compare and classify; understands cause and effect (e.g. can understand why..., because..., if..., then...). These skills lead into problem solving activities. Child will attempt to explain how or why events occur/occurred.

9. Prediction of events: child is able to discuss what is likely to happen in familiar events that will take place in the near future, and the possible outcomes of stories, social behaviour, etc.

10. Planning: child can contribute to discussion to plan future activity considering equipment needed and steps required to complete the task.

11. Imagining: child is able to invent make-believe objects, actions and events, to tell stories and to extend his/her own thinking and feeling.

12. Instructing: child is able to give simple instructions to adult or peer, e.g. to play simple game, find hidden object, draw specific picture.

Profile of language use: junior

1. Initiation of conversation with unfamiliar adults and children: child has the confidence to initiate conversations with unfamiliar people by commenting, volunteering information or asking questions.

2. Projection of thoughts and feelings: child can consider and describe the thoughts and feelings that might be felt by self and others in range of situations, familiar and less familiar.

3. Instructing: child is able to give a sequence of instruction to adult or peer, e.g. to play a game, draw a specific picture, build a particular model from Lego, draw route on map, or shape/object on squared paper following compass directions.

4. Explaining: explains activities, events, own actions clearly and concisely.

5. Imaginative use of language: child uses wide range of vocabulary to express imaginative thinking in talking, drama, puppetry, writing, etc.

6. Extended use of questions: child can contribute to discussion and devise a set of questions to pursue a line of enquiry.

7. Planning: child is able to think ahead to decide equipment and steps required to complete task; can describe to others.

8. Hypothesising: child is able to suggest possible explanations of events.

9. Inferring and deducing: child's questions, answers, comments, explanations, etc. show evidence of deduction and inference.

10. Reflecting on and exploring language: child shows interest in language by recognising and appreciating puns, understanding and making simple jokes, participating in activities for extending vocabulary, etc.

11. Presenting sequenced oral account: child can deliver an oral story or account of events in clear and concise chronological order.

12. Giving opinions: child will give reasoned opinion on range of experiences, activities, issues; will consider alternative opinions and discuss.

(Locke 1985)

The Websters' *Profiles of Development* (1995) provides a developmental check-list against which to assess pupil progress. The section on 'communication' provides items under the following headings.

- Pragmatics: functional communication.
- Interaction: pre-verbal stages to conversation.
- Listening: use of hearing.
- Receptive language.
- Expressive language.

- Clarity of speech.

- Finger spelling.

- Signing.

- Hearing aids.

As an example, items from 'receptive language' include the following.

Item 1: points to familiar thing when named (spoken or signed), e.g. 'Show me the cat/ball/book'.

Item 19: selects two real objects by use, e.g. 'Which do we drink with?'

Item 35: responds to simple sentences with prepositions such as under/near/beside/with/through.

Item 58: understands the passive voice in conversation, e.g. 'the girl was kicked by the horse'.

A detailed language assessment scheme has been developed by staff including speech therapists at Gap House School. This scheme seeks to provide a comprehensive diagnostic assessment which covers the following areas:

- *underlying factors* (e.g. attention control, auditory discrimination, auditory memory, visual perception);

- *structure of language* (syntax, morphology, etc.);

- *cognitive use of language* (concept development, word relationships, verbal reasoning, etc.);

- *social use of language* (non-verbal, turn-taking, conversational flow, etc.);

- *interaction* (communicative intent, relationships, etc.);

- *imagination* (role play, humour, etc.).

There are various commercially produced assessment schemes which teachers may find useful to inform target setting and strategy development for young KS1/2 pupils. These include:

- *Teaching Talking – The Interaction Screen* by Ann Locke and Maggie Beech; published by NFER-Nelson, this test is based on the observation and recording of behaviours which occur in an interactional social setting.

- *Teaching Talking – The Primary Screen* by Ann Locke and Maggie Beech. This screen is based on observation and identifies difficulties in social and spoken language. It comprises:

  – emerging language development record (2–5 years);
  – maturing language record (5–11yrs);
  – play and social development chart;
  – listening and understanding chart;
  – speaking and listening chart.

- *AFASIC Speech and Language Screening Test for 4–5 year olds*. Published by LDA. This records:

  - language structure (sound articulation and grammar);
  - language content (attention and comprehension, vocabulary and expressive language).

- *AFASIC Speech and Language Screening Test for 6–10 year olds*. This records:

  - response to sound;
  - movement and motor skills;
  - cognitive processes;
  - errors in sound;
  - communication;
  - play and recreation;
  - vocabulary;
  - grammar.

- *Renfrew Action Picture Test* (Catharine Renfrew), published by Winslow. A standardised test to evaluate the information given and grammatical structures used in samples of spoken language.

- *The Renfrew Language Scales*, published by Winslow. A standardised test for children aged 3–8 yrs to assess their word finding vocabulary.

- *British Picture Vocabulary Scales* (BPVS), published by NFER-Nelson. A standardised test to assess receptive vocabulary.

- *South Tyneside Assessment of Syntactic Structures* (STASS) by Susan Armstrong and Maureen Ainley. This test aims to provide a rapid assessment of possible areas of difficulty within a child's expressive language.

National Literacy Strategy (DfEE 1997)

From September 1998 onwards schools are expected to respond to the National Literacy Strategy. While there is as yet no specific guidance for SEN pupils, the National Literacy Strategy stated that SEN pupils' literacy needs would be met through IEP provision. The framework for teaching issued to schools uses the following structure:

word level: phonics, spelling and vocabulary;

sentence level: grammar and punctuation;

text level: comprehension and composition.

This structure has particular implications for pupils with speech and language difficulties. The daily literacy hour, which is central to the framework for teaching (p. 9), is structured to include:

- 15 minutes of whole-class teaching directed towards shared text work involving a balance of reading and writing;

- 15 minutes of focused word work;

- 20 minutes of group and independent work on reading, writing or word work;

- 10 minutes during which the whole class review, reflect on and consolidate teaching points covered in the lesson.

Given this framework it might be helpful for schools to consider using an assessment procedure which is linked to the following 'structure' of language:

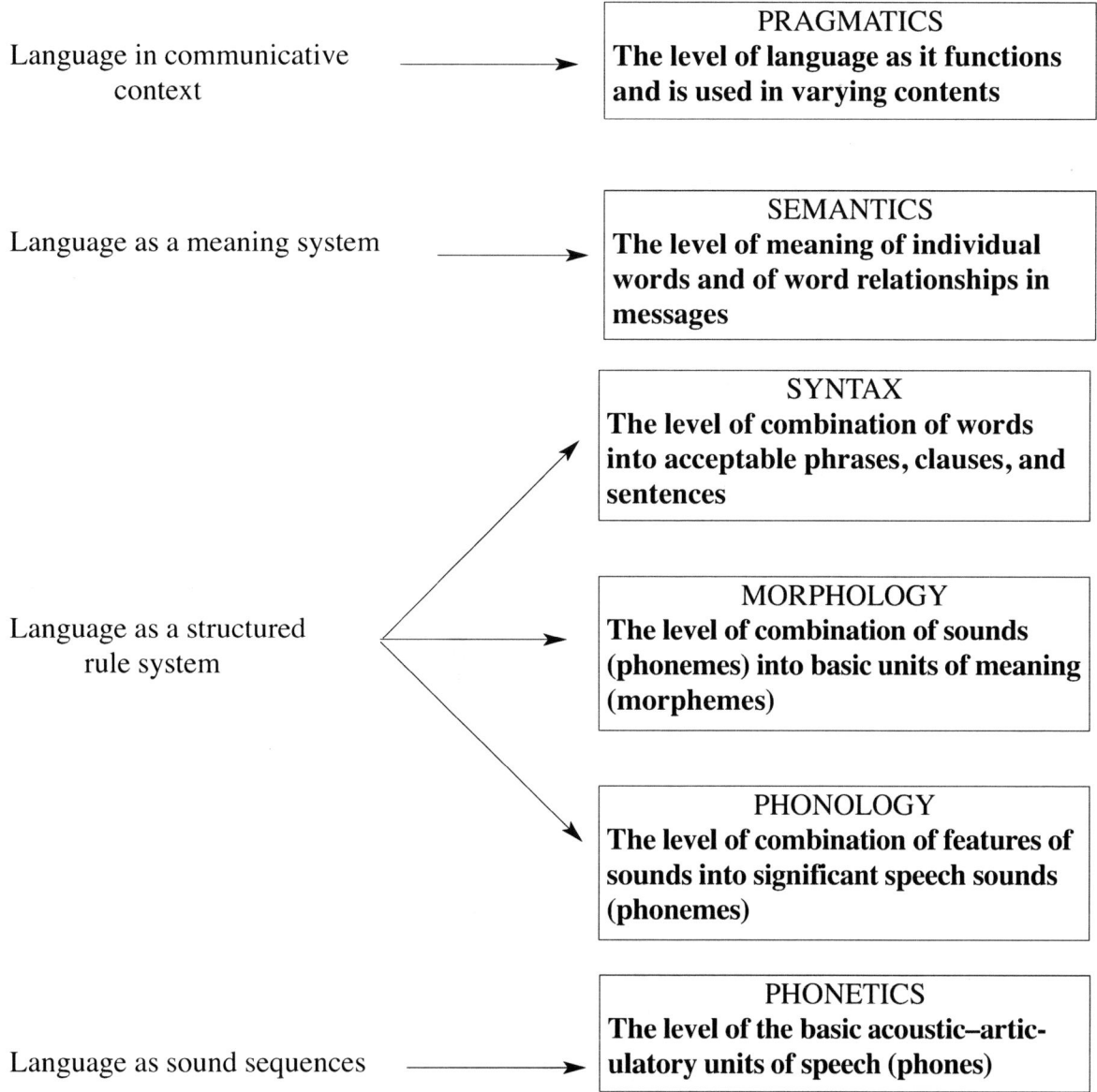

Language in communicative context → **PRAGMATICS**
The level of language as it functions and is used in varying contents

Language as a meaning system → **SEMANTICS**
The level of meaning of individual words and of word relationships in messages

Language as a structured rule system → **SYNTAX**
The level of combination of words into acceptable phrases, clauses, and sentences

MORPHOLOGY
The level of combination of sounds (phonemes) into basic units of meaning (morphemes)

PHONOLOGY
The level of combination of features of sounds into significant speech sounds (phonemes)

Language as sound sequences → **PHONETICS**
The level of the basic acoustic–articulatory units of speech (phones)

Example of typical presenting features of delay v. disorder at the various speech and language levels

DELAY		DISORDER

DELAY		DISORDER
Socially very immature.	PRAGMATICS	Inappropriate social/verbal behaviour. Difficulty making relationships. Inappropriate stress and intonation.
Limited comprehension and expression of words.	SEMANTICS	Word finding difficulties. Frequent changes of subject. Lack of content words.
Using sentences appropriate to a much younger child.	SYNTAX	Inappropriate use of word order. Lack of grammatical function words.
Not using word endings appropriate to chronological age.	MORPHOLOGY	Inappropriate use of word endings/no word endings. No tense changes.
Uses typically immature sound substitutions or omissions but can usually produce the target sounds in isolation. Errors are consistent.	PHONOLOGY	Uses deviant sound substitutions or omissions. Errors may be inconsistent.
Slow acquisition of articulatory movements required for speech sounds.	ARTICULATION	Limited acquisition of articulatory movements required for speech sounds.

Given this structure of language it is possible for teachers to design a framework for assessment of pupils with speech and language difficulties which is consistent with the notion of IEP planning to support pupils in the context of the Literacy Strategy. The following one is a general check-list which may serve to screen for difficulties linked to the structure of language:

Check-list for class teachers
Name:.........................   Class:....................   Date:...........................

PRAGMATICS	SEMANTICS
Does the pupil ask relevant questions/make appropriate responses?	Does the pupil exhibit word finding difficulties?
Does he/she interrupt or change the topic of conversation?	Does he/she give unexpected responses to questions?
Does he/she use inappropriate volume, intonation or unusual voice?	Does he interpret words literally and exhibit problems in understanding subject specific language, e.g. in maths?
Does he/she laugh at the wrong times/appear cheeky or rude?	Does he/she need spoken language to be repeated for it to be understood?
Does he/she tend to talk at rather than to teacher and peers?	Does he/she have difficulty 'thinking' of what to say/write?
Does the pupil take turns?	Does he use circumlocutions (i.e. 'the thing that you write with' for 'pen') with many 'you know's', etc.?
Does the pupil exhibit limited eye contact?	Does he/she have difficulty predicting 'what comes next' when reading for meaning?
	Can he/she follow instructions without prompting?
PHONETICS	MORPHOLOGY
Does the pupil exhibit difficulty in making sound for speech?	Does the pupil use incorrect tenses, e.g. 'I goed home'? Does he misuse endings: 'I saw two bus'?
SYNTAX	PHONOLOGY
Does the child leave out words in a sentence or use telegrammatic speech?	Can the pupil recognise and generate rhyme?
Does he/she put the words in the correct order within the sentence?	Can he/she clap out or tap the syllables in a word?
Does he/she use parts of speech (e.g. pronouns) correctly?	Does he/she leave out syllables/sounds within a word?

The following format for classroom based assessment may be particularly useful for IEP planning and evaluation and may help to lead teachers into using certain strategies which have a 'goodness of fit' with those needed to support the meeting of National Literacy targets.

Classroom analysis of speech, language and communication difficulties

Name................. Class............... Date............ Teacher...........................

Highlight relevant BEHAVIOURS and add any others observed; highlight the appropriate LANGUAGE COMPONENT. Use the suggested STRATEGIES and highlight those found to be particularly effective. Add any others found to be successful.

Language component	Observed behaviours	Suggested strategies
Phonetics: the articulation of units of speech.	Inability to enunciate some speech sounds. Confusion between similarly produced speech sounds, e.g. voiced and voiceless 't/d','k/g'.	• Model correct usage by extending what has been said in the correct form. • **Seek advice** from speech therapist on best approach, i.e. use of cued articulation to show production of sound, etc.
Phonology/phonological awareness: the awareness of sounds within words.	Difficulty in generating rhyme. Difficulty breaking down words into syllables (segmenting words into phonemes). Difficulty in identifying phonemes in speech and writing. Difficulty with blending phonemes into words.	• Music based activities which encourage listening, recognition and generating: high/low; short/long; loud/soft. • Auditory discrimination games: sound lotto. • Listening to rhymes – picking out non-rhyming word. • Clapping out patterns, i.e. 3 claps for elephant. • Use multi-sensory techniques – listen to word, look at visual pattern, trace in sand, say out loud, etc. • Supported generation of rhyme (cued?): h*at*, c*at*, m*at*, etc.

Language component	Observed behaviours	Suggested strategies
Morphology: the combination of sound into basic units of meaning (e.g. one morpheme: 'house'; two morphemes: house/s; three: house/keep/ing).	Word endings not used or inappropriately used (in relation to chronological age). Tenses not used or incorrect.	• Model language: e.g. if child said: 'I rided my bike yesterday' response could be 'So you *rode* your bike yesterday – where did you go?' • Don't correct. • Use visual cues to correct word endings, etc. – colour code – use puzzle shapes so that pupil can recognise and fit correct ending, etc.
Syntax: the grammatical relationships between words, phrases and clauses.	Use of immature sentences (i.e. two word 'gone pen', etc.); inappropriate use of word order. Lack of or limited use of grammatical function words, e.g. articles, connectives, etc. Misuse or omission of pronouns. To predict words when reading which will make sense.	• Aim to improve language through: commentary on child's activity; reading stories; use of cued short requests which convey grammatically correct order. • Use of stories or familiar incidents (e.g. video of football game for: who? why? what? when? where? questions and answers, etc.). • Sort written words into correct order, e.g. boy, the, head, on, his, put, hat, his. • Object hunt with clues: **on** the shelf, **under** the bin, etc. • Use written format to stress conventional features and grammatical features, e.g. question marks, commas, link to oral speech pauses, intonation, etc.
Semantics: the meaning of individual words and of word relationships.	Difficulty with expressive language. Difficulty in understanding language. Word finding difficulties. Inappropriate responses to questions.	• Use visual language strategies. • Use short, clear sentences spoken slowly. • Make implicit explicit. • Teach through practical experience.

Language component	Observed behaviours	Suggested strategies
	Difficulty with classification (i.e. use of concept words – 'fruit'). Literal understanding. Difficulty with concepts of time, space, comparison, etc. Need for time to process and respond to information. Often exhibit sequencing and short-term memory difficulties.	• Use objects and pictures to reinforce key words. • Make use of ICT multimedia software for language and reading development. • Build on language the child already has.
Pragmatics: language for communication, 'social use of language', how language functions in varying contexts.	Talks 'at' rather than 'to' the listener. Difficulty in 'reading' social situation – does not heed social conventions of classroom, e.g. may talk at same time as teacher, interrupt, not take turns, etc. Literal response, e.g. 'have you finished talking?'; answer: 'no, not yet'. May seek to reduce stimulation by avoidance, e.g. limited or absent eye contact, attention directed away from social activities towards solitary repetitive activity. May talk about a topic over and over again even though listener has heard about it previously. May have limited attention span at times, rigidity of attention at other times.	• Make implicit social conventions of classroom explicit (when we are in class we sit down, etc. via use of social stories, etc.). • Try to understand why the pupil is responding as he does – if social stimulation is excessive and frightening then ensure own space free from distractions for working. • Use visual timetables and TEACCH strategies. • Teach turn-taking and other social behaviour in structured safe setting initially, i.e. 'circle time'. • Use written instructions, visual prompts. • Make use of IT which is impersonal, etc. to teach new skills before transfer to social setting. • If changes to routine have to be made try to explain beforehand emphasising the full sequence of events: e.g. 'we are going to the swimming pool today. *When we have finished swimming we will come back to school'*.

In summary, it is important that schools consider the need for Code of Practice assessment within the whole-school framework for assessment. Some frameworks have been described above – it may be that primary schools would prefer to adapt and extent baseline assessment within the 'structure of language' framework so that there is an assessment system in place which supports the National Literacy Strategy. IEP provision for SEN pupils will naturally *emerge* from this framework and can be assessed in relation to the assessment framework.

Secondary schools may prefer to adopt the National Curriculum English framework against which to compare pupil progress and set targets.

The frameworks were not designed for pupils with speech and language difficulties and as such have limitations – however, it is better for teachers to work from a curricular linked framework than to seek out 'tests' of normative function which may serve to provide targets which isolate the pupil from both the curriculum and the social world of his/her peers. Of the frameworks described above only the English National Curriculum 'speaking and listening' 'key skills' highlights the need for varying attentional styles to be consolidated and developed through a range of language experiences and opportunities. Curricular frameworks in general are characterised by descriptors which can be used to plan programmes of study but which lack the precision needed to provide 'diagnostic' assessment necessary for target setting and strategy design. Teachers have to move forward a step from descriptive generic reporting towards an analysis which enables them to answer the question: 'What does this information tell me about the pupil's need for different or extra provision?' IEP planning for pupils with speech and language difficulties is essentially an ongoing time framed problem-solving activity not a discrete response to an identified pupil deficit.

Writing targets: Principles

...central to the notion of IEP planning is the principle of setting learning outcomes in advance as targets to be attained within set time periods (written as what is to be learned not how to increase the learning opportunities).

SENJIT Schools Policy Pack (NCB 1995)

Purpose of targets

- Provide a focus for *coordinated educational effort* because everyone involved shares a common goal.

- Strengthen the links between policy, planning and provision.

- Provide a means for assessing the effectiveness of provision.

- Support staff development in relation to SEN.

- Provide realistic challenges.

- Provide more rigorous criteria for the reporting of progress.

- Establish agreed priorities of need.

Targets arise from the assessment of pupil progress within the curriculum and their individual profile of strengths and weaknesses. The *educational effectiveness* of targets rests on their design and selection as well as the shared belief of those involved that they are realistic and worthwhile. The setting of targets can provide a focus for the collaborative educational effort and may involve parents and learners in target setting. Furthermore, planning to achieve targets can direct attention to the efficient use of resources and the direct linking of teaching to learning outcomes.

The achievement of targets can be a measure of the effectiveness of IEPs, and therefore, of the school's SEN provision. It is important to remember, however, that targets do not exist independently. Setting them does not in itself achieve anything, neither does it necessarily result in effective teaching.

Possible pitfalls in writing targets for pupils with speech and language difficulties

- Language and communication are characterised by their flexibility and responsiveness. IEP targets are characterised by their specificity. Sometimes targets set do not take account of the medium- or long-term social, emotional and learning needs of the pupil – thus once achieved they do not have an 'impact' on pupil progress. 'A key feature of effective school policies on special needs were: practical strategies for the identification and assessment of pupils' short, medium and long-term difficulties, with clear expectations and advice for staff on writing IEPs' (OFSTED 1996).

• They can lead to a narrow focus for intervention which does not link access and entitlement to the National Curriculum, i.e. they are 'exclusive' rather than 'inclusive'.

• They could lead to a false picture of 'effectiveness', i.e. many narrow targets achieved over a short period of time may not be synonymous with real educational progress.

• They could lead to the assumption that language outcomes can be broken down into small steps which exist out of context. By focusing solely on these steps one could lose sight of the overall outcome and might then believe that the steps themselves, when achieved, are the outcome.

• There is a danger that available resources may dictate targets rather than needs.

• They may be used manipulatively, e.g. if a school feels that a pupil needs additional resources then targets could be selected to evidence 'slow' progress. Alternatively 'progress' could be falsely speeded up by the selection of targets which are relatively easy for the pupil to achieve.

• The achievement of targets might become the *only* indicator of educational progress.

• Targets might become linked to 'category' of need and be generated from lists of targets available from commercial schemes. This assumes that pupils who share a label, e.g. 'autistic', also share deficits and/or needs. The setting of an IEP target may serve to emphasis that the 'target' is the responsibility of the child. The achievement of language and communication targets, e.g. 'to take turns', 'to seek clarification' and to 'sustain joint attention', etc., does require action and response from those involved in the language exchange.

Currently there is an emphasis on SMART (*s*pecific, *m*anageable, *a*chievable, *r*elevant and *t*imed targets; Lloyd and Berthelot 1992), with some LEAs prescribing that targets *must* fit these criteria. It should be stressed that this emphasis has sometimes fostered practice which is at odds with the principles of the Code of Practice in that it has lessened learning opportunities for the child.

Setting learning outcomes in advance as targets can be a sound principle for some aspects of teaching, particularly when the content of what has to be taught is highly structured. However, task analysis undertaken without reference to the effect of social context will provide achievable but not necessarily relevant targets. The currently favoured model is to provide teachers with guidance on how to write targets and then to provide them with lists of targets linked to categories of need. This method could be useful as a way of improving teacher competence in planning for SEN teaching, provided the aim is not simply to achieve 'technical competence' so that the IEP procedure can continue to be seen to be operational. The design and selection of educationally relevant targets require more than technical competence. They require at the very least a knowledge and understanding of individual differences in learning style, an understanding of the substantive issues surrounding the acquisition and use of language and an awareness of the effect of different teaching approaches on pupil progress and of the importance of monitoring pupil response to his/her IEP.

Types of targets

It might be useful to provide teachers with a taxonomy of 'targets'. These could fall under three categories as shown below.

- Direct linkage: learning outcome = target.
- Flexible linkage: target = range of possible learning outcomes.
- Indirect linkage: target = an outcome which can be recognised but not prescribed.

Targets may be classified as:

- 'access targets';
- 'process targets';
- 'response/interactive targets'.

	Target = direct linkage (learning outcome = target)	Target = flexible linkage (range of possible learning outcomes)	Indirect linkage (outcome can be recognised but not prescribed)
ACCESS: active listening, attentional styles, asking questions, monitoring comprehension, etc.	Will look at teacher when she uses his/her name.	Will make it known to the teacher if he/she does not understand.	Will self-direct his attention to the task given to him.
PROCESS: sort relevant from irrelevant, relate to previous experience, categorise, memorise, etc.	Will listen to and repeat instructions given personally to him.	Will record information in a note book so that material is available in a permanent form.	Will be able to demonstrate that he has retained key information from the lesson.
RESPONSE: coherence, social convention, clarity, relevance.	Will select correct item in response to verbal request: 'give me the blue pencil'.	Will evidence 'turn-taking' (could be in PE, or waiting for teacher to finish talking etc.).	Will show increasing confidence in relation to communication with peers.

In summary

Teachers may need to use SMART targets for their particular subject area. Targets should ideally be set by those who understand both the pupil needs and the curricular demands. In the case of speech, language and communication difficulties it is important that subject teachers make explicit the vocabulary and language demands of their particular subject (e.g. literature: the need to be able to perceive other people's perspective, the language of maths, etc.) so that need for 'extra or different' provision can be targeted.

However, as with all educational practice, an exclusive reliance on one type of target linked to reductionist approaches is not synonymous with effective teaching. Teachers need to develop their understanding of the relationship between targeting, teaching, learning and responding. To avoid the pitfalls inherent in adopting one fixed approach to target setting it may be useful for teachers to consider a balanced educational diet of targets.

Targets need to be relevant to the pupil. It is helpful if parents and pupils contribute to target setting particularly at the initial stages of planning. Teachers are naturally concerned with 'subject' targets and there may well be pressure to concentrate on literacy, numeracy and behavioural targets. Parents and pupils may have different priorities which may be equally effective in terms of promoting progress via an improvement in the pupil's social relationships and emotional wellbeing.

What can be counted might not count.

What counts might not be countable.

(Einstein)

Target setting: Institutional self-review

- Do the targets address identified concerns?

- Are targets achievable within a defined time scale for the child?

- Do targets translate into educationally relevant outcomes?

- Do they provide challenges for the pupil?

- Do they create a direct link between planning and provision?

- Do they reduce complexity?

- Do they prioritise aims?

- Are they easily understood by all involved in the IEP?

- To what extent has the design of targets involved all concerned (i.e. pupil and parent)?

- Do they serve to increase the learning opportunity for the child?

- Do targets identify the 'different and extra'?

- Do they avoid isolating and excluding the pupil?

- Are targets linked to long- and medium-term aims?

- Is their achievement likely to have an 'impact' on progress?

- Are they relevant to the pupil in terms of positively affecting social interaction and emotional wellbeing?

Monitoring: Principles

Why do you need to monitor IEPs?

For the IEP to work it needs to be monitored to ensure that the plan is being put into practice and is making use of the strategies and resources that have been identified in the IEP. The IEP states what is *different* or *extra* that is needed. This needs to be monitored by those involved. It is an ongoing dynamic process not a retrospective record of failure.

Monitoring arrangements should relate to the information recorded on the IEP documentation. These arrangements are most successful when they are integrated into existing whole-school assessment and monitoring procedures and when the whole school takes on the responsibility.

	The sum of all IEPs	IEP
Learner	Not applicable	Is my IEP helping me?
LSA/CA	Am I managing the IEP process for all my pupils? Am I making efficient use of resources?	How effective is my delivery of the IEP? How well is the pupil responding? What adjustments could I make?
Class or subject teacher	Am I managing the IEP process for all my pupils and the staff involved? Am I making efficient use of resources (human and otherwise)?	How effective is the (or my) delivery of the IEP?
SENCO	How effective is the IEP procedure for pupils in this school? How manageable are the IEP procedures in this school? What are the implications for whole-school development?	(Does the IEP procedure conform to COP (and LEA) requirements?) Does the IEP need to be changed? Are the review dates being adhered to? Is everyone concerned clear about their roles and responsibilities? Have sufficient assessment data been collected to inform the next stage of action?
Outside agencies	How many IEPs is our agency concerned with in the school? Is our involvement with the school's IEPs effective and what are our resource implications?	Is our advice being effectively applied via delivery of the pupil's IEP? Is the pupil making progress as anticipated?
Parents		Is my child making progress? Is he/she receiving the provision agreed on the IEP? Is my contribution valued and effective?
SMT	Do the school's IEP procedures conform to the COP and LEA requirements? Is the IEP procedure being effectively managed in the school? Are the pupils making progress? Do the school's IEP procedures conform to the COP and LEA requirements? Are the IEP procedures consistent with the school's SEN policy? Are the pupils receiving the provision described on their IEP? What are the implications for: ● school development; ● budget and resource allocation; ● staff development and training?	Are individual pupils making progress as expected? Are there problems with any individual IEPs which may be addressed by the SMT (e.g. parental concerns)? Are strategies cited on individual IEPs consistent with school policy for language, behaviour and communication?

Roles and responsibilities

The IEP can be seen as being supported by a team of all those who are involved. The child and parents are central to this team and should be encouraged to participate as far as they are able. The monitoring process will be carried out by the different members of the IEP team at varying frequencies and for different purposes (see Figure 4). The SENCO acts as a facilitator – all information is filtered through the SENCO.

The IEP is a *brief working plan* that may need to be altered as a result of monitoring.

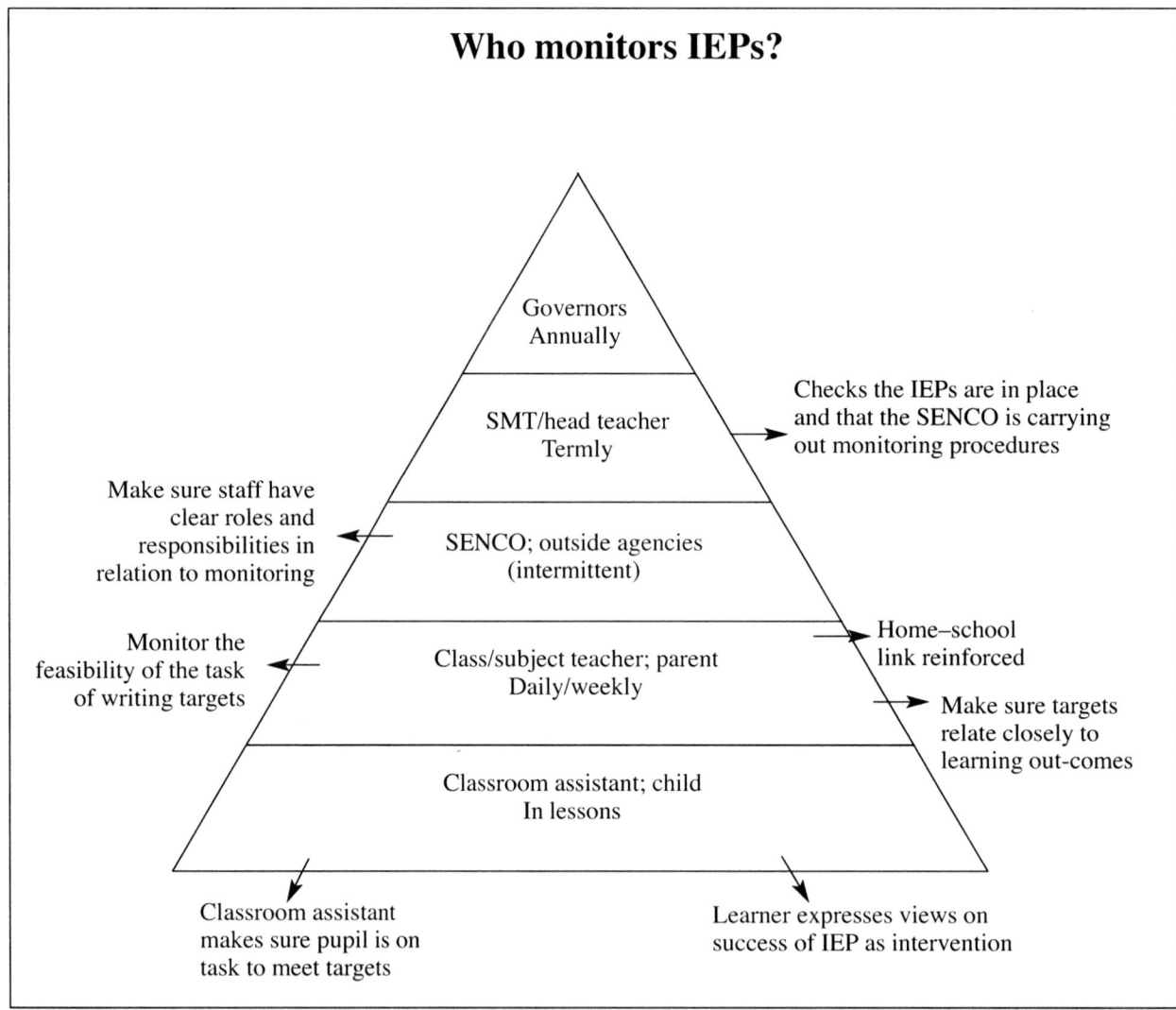

Who monitors IEPs?

Governors
Annually

SMT/head teacher
Termly

SENCO; outside agencies
(intermittent)

Class/subject teacher; parent
Daily/weekly

Classroom assistant; child
In lessons

Checks the IEPs are in place and that the SENCO is carrying out monitoring procedures

Make sure staff have clear roles and responsibilities in relation to monitoring

Monitor the feasibility of the task of writing targets

Home–school link reinforced

Make sure targets relate closely to learning out-comes

Classroom assistant makes sure pupil is on task to meet targets

Learner expresses views on success of IEP as intervention

Figure 4

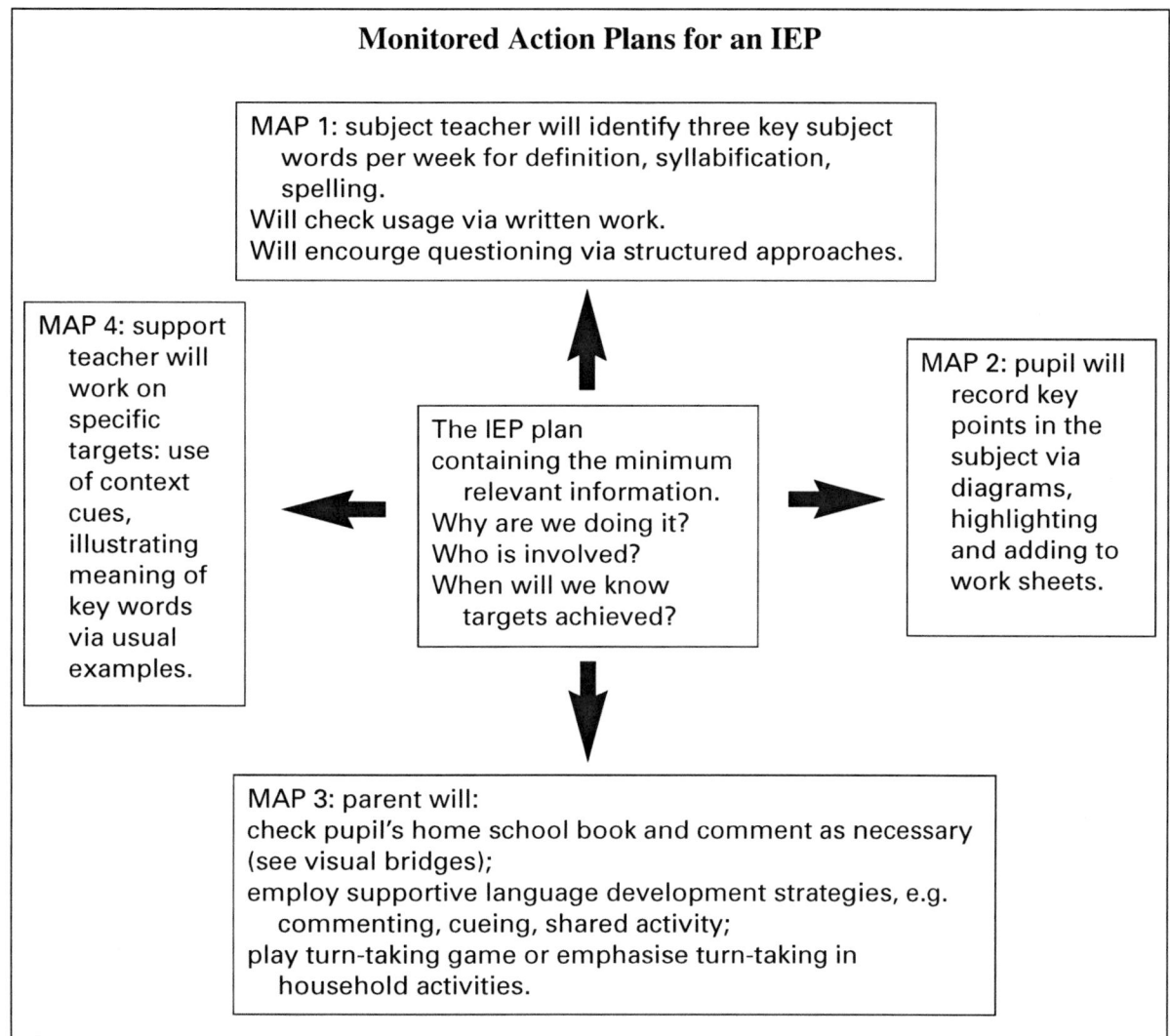

Figure 5

Figure 5 seeks to show how 'paperwork' for IEP planning can be reduced. The idea is that everyone involved in the IEP is clear about their role in meeting IEP targets and monitoring pupil response. The individual concerned is aware of their MAP (Monitored Action Plan) and takes responsibility for it. All that is needed is for each individual to provide feedback at the required intervals and to communicate back to the central IEP if changes are needed.

Monitoring: Institutional self-review

- Do your monitoring procedures enable you to establish the content of the link between the written IEP and classroom practice?

- Does the monitoring inform those concerned about the effectiveness of strategies employed?

- Are all those involved in the IEP process aware of which targets they are working on and how to record progress in relation to those targets?

- Is the working document clear and easy to use?

- Does it tie in with established routines and procedures within the school?

- Is the IEP linked in with planning and assessment at all levels?

- Is time allocated to the monitoring of IEPs?

- Does the monitoring of IEPs result in action? If it doesn't then it is not worth doing.

- Is the monitoring process manageable?

Monitoring: Ideas for action

Table to show how sessional/LSA monitoring might take place

Positive responses: strengths	Difficulties encountered	Action points
Attended well when material presented visually.	Pupil regularly needed instructions simplified or repeated.	Adjust vocabulary; speak slower; shorten instructions; use visual cues; cue in 'joint attention'; check task difficulty – adjust.
Took turns with peer when using computer game.	Had difficulty sequencing ideas. Started task then did not know how to finish.	Give task overview – and what is required. Help with planning, using visual aid to allow pupil to self-check when he has completed each step.
Looked at adult for help when he/she did not understand.	Could respond correctly sometimes – not others.	Check comprehension by using recognition response initially before asking child to generate own response. Record and reward correct response. Model correct response.
Brought in home school book and was able to say what he had done at the weekend by using photograph cues.	Did not initiate any communication.	Would he prefer to work in a small group? Give pupil 'conversation script' which he follows; then ask him to write script; then cue in when it is his turn to 'start' conversation. Supply list of conventional questions, social phrases for him/her to select from.
Remembered to bring items needed for lesson.	Uses grammatically immature sentences.	Model and emphasise grammatically correct format – use written word to give visual emphasis to sentence structure. Colour code part of speech – get pupil to order correctly. See if he/she can *recognise* correct/incorrect format.
How can these be built upon for next session?	How does this affect achievement of targets?	Teaching points?

Schools can develop their own monitoring sheets which require staff simply to highlight or record strengths or difficulties and teaching points.

This is a generic monitoring sheet for those involved in delivering the IEP to draw attention to the need to build on pupil response and adjust delivery accordingly.

PERSON RESPONSIBLE AND PURPOSE OF MONITORING	General questions asked by the person who delivers the IEP concerning the child's response to his/her IEP	Task: possible action	Strategy resource: possible action	Setting/context: possible action
Learning support Child in class Parent. 'Did today's session achieve its learning outcomes? If not, what changes may be appropriate?'	Is the child interested and on task for most of the session?	Can I make the task more relevant?	Can I get the child more *actively* involved by personalising the task?	Change grouping: would pupil rather work with a peer?
	Is he able to understand the task? (i.e. access)?	Should I break the task down into smaller steps? Reduce the speed of presentation.	Change mode of presentation from verbal to visual.	Would it be appropriate for me to give the pupil first hand experience via school visit?
	Is he able to process the information?	Is the task linked to something he/she knows already?	Can I get the child to *actively* process material by giving assistance to study skills, and emphasising metacognition?	Would a collaborative small group setting be more appropriate than 1:1 support?
	Is he able to give appropriate responses to the task?	Assist with responding in small steps – allow sufficient *time* for a response to be generated. Clarify success and failure? Highlight key areas of the task to direct child's attention.	Is the required answer simply too difficult, i.e. should I 'meet him half-way' by asking for a recognition response before I ask for recall? Or should the correct response be modelled first, etc?	Would it help initially if joint or parallel activity was involved to reduce any fear of the individual

On the next two pages is an IEP format which incorporates a monitoring sheet to ensure that monitoring at various levels has occurred. It is an example of an IEP which could be used in the primary or secondary setting. The detail is limited to essentials for monitoring collective IEPs. The tear-off signed slip serves to trigger those involved. The IEP is sent to all those involved and evaluated by the check sheet on the reverse.

Distribution: | E: | M: | Sc: | H: | G: | MFL: | Mus: | Tech: | Art: | PE: | Pastoral: | Parent: | Individual: |

MinIEP

Name: _____

Stage 2 ☐ 3 ☐

Class: _____

Class teacher: _____

Yr: _____

Professionals involved:

EWO ☐ SLT ☐ Medical ☐ CA ☐
Physio ☐ OT ☐ Learning support ☐

Current date / /

Date of next review (usually a term after current date) / /

Parents' names: _____

Other _____

Key concerns arising from assessment:

Targets (agreed identified outcomes):

Strategies:

Resources:

Outcomes achieved: | Date: | Action (change strategies, alter targets or resources): |

....

Agreed Action Plan (who, what, when, where and for how long): note action, tear off and sign, return to SEN clerical
Name of child:

Signature   **Role**, e.g. teacher, parent, subject or special support   **Date:**

55

Check-list for monitoring IEPs at an institutional level

Role	Frequency	What is monitored?
Learner	Daily [ ] On each task [ ]	e.g. success, difficulty of task
LSA / CA	Each session [ ] Daily [ ]	Self-help skills, motivation and time on task; response to strategy
CT/ST	Daily [ ] Each lesson [ ]	e.g. success of strategies in relation to targets
SENCO	Checking and sampling (state when)	The effectiveness of the design and delivery of the IEP
Outside agencies	Intermittent (state when)	The effectiveness and take-up of their advice and intervention
Parents	Daily [ ] Weekly [ ]	Home-school links, homework, rewarding progress at school and learner response to parental involvement
SMT	Termly [ ]	Efficiency of IEPs and implications for School Development Plan; efficient use of resources
Governors	Annually [ ]	Goodness of fit of IEP procedures within the SEN policy; requirements of the Code and resource implications; efficient use of resources

IEP evaluation	Yes	No	Partially
Are the targets addressing areas of concern?			
Are the targets achievable?			
Are the targets setting challenges?			
Are the strategies appropriate for the targets?			
Are the strategies being delivered effectively?			
Is regular monitoring taking place?			
Is the Action Plan/IEP manageable?			

Implication for action	Action to be taken	By whom

Signed: Date:

Please return to the SENCO/Clerical by the review date

Strategies within IEPs: Principles

Few teachers use many of them	Many teachers use a few of them

(Hodgon 1995)

It may be that only a few strategies are needed for effective learning provided they are applied and monitored consistently. The skill is in making time to consider how strategies can be applied with an individual learner within the constraints of the classroom and the school.

We have found that some SENCOs considered part of their function was to provide 'strategies for all occasions'. However, many teachers have found it difficult to tailor these 'off-the-shelf' strategies to the identified needs of their learners. The SENCO role has developed to support teachers in applying and monitoring strategies as part of ongoing classroom assessment.

The sheer number and range of unfamiliar sounding strategies might appear threatening and de-skilling to many teachers. In response to this, we have attempted to establish the underpinning strategies upon which all the rest are based. We tentatively put forward ten key strategies which underlie the dimensions of differentiation. Individualisation may be based upon these. They are a framework for a teacher to consider what they can change in their teaching. We further suggest that this approach addresses the criticism that 'IEPs lead to the creation of deficits within the child'. These strategies focus upon what can be changed within the school to support the next stage of learning for the child.

The 10 key strategies(?)

Strategy 1:   Clarity of what is expected

Strategy 2:   Predictability/novelty

Strategy 3:   Affirmation/criticism (reward system)

Strategy 4:   Interaction/group work

Strategy 5:   Available time for tasks (workload)

Strategy 6:   Negotiation/conflict (choice)

Strategy 7:   Level of work (complexity)

Strategy 8:   Modality

Strategy 9:   Reading/language demand

Strategy 10:   Attention (given or expected)

Holistic language interventions: Principles

For children with language and communication difficulties, a number of strategies/ approaches have been developed and marketed. Each approach has a set of implicit or explicit values underpinning its use and may cover one aspect of language and communication development. We have attempted to provide an overarching framework to consider these approaches using the ten key strategies.

At the centre of this model are levels of attention that are needed for language acquisition and use. It follows that strategies for developing attentional styles are implemented within the three areas of language (see Figure 6).

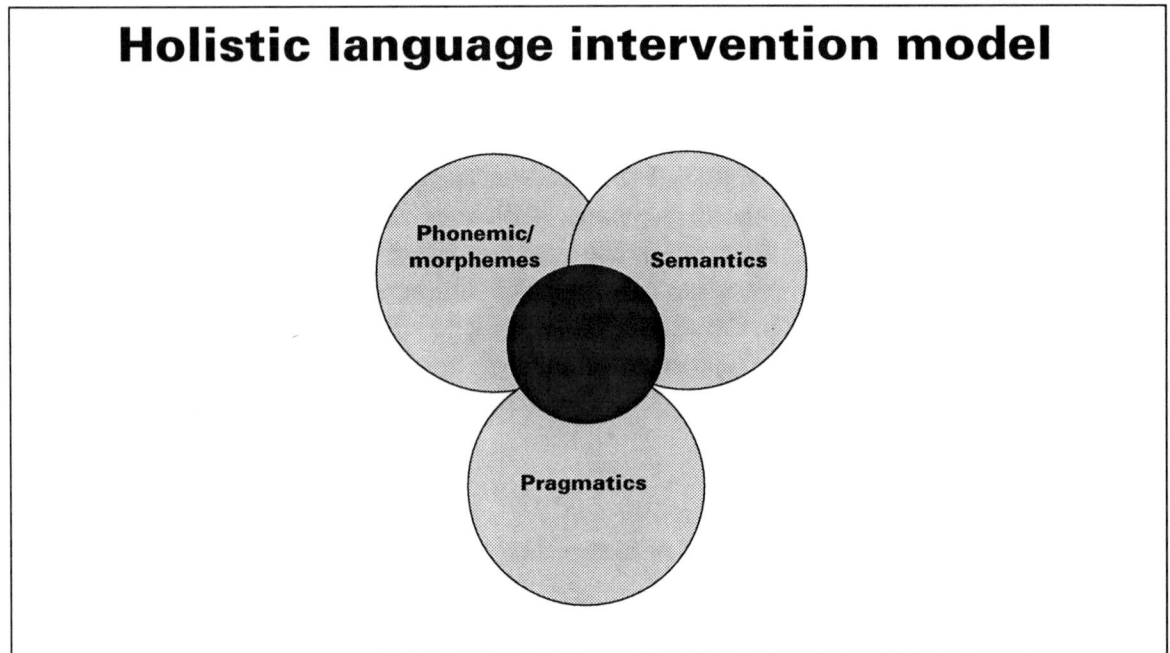

Figure 6

Attentional styles

When children acquire language in a natural setting the adult supplies both context and cues which enable the development of a range of attentional styles needed for social and cognitive functioning. Underlying this is the ability to focus, sustain, redirect and share attention so the individual can learn from, and respond to, their environment. In the early years this occurs in a supportive setting with adult carers and siblings, whereas a formal school setting demands skilled performance in the full range of attentional styles.

However, by assessing the repertoire of attentional styles employed by the learner in a range of settings it is possible to reduce mismatch between task demand and attentional competency. There has been a move away from a child deficit approach to attention focused upon time on task. This has led towards a consideration of the interactive nature of shared and cued attention.

Levels of attention

Reynell (1978) has identified stages in the development of attention control and linked these with the development of school learning and language. These have been usefully summarised by Martin and Miller (1996):

Stage 1
This is the type of attention observable in young babies. They are extremely distractible and pay only momentary attention to the main stimulus of the moment. For example, the introduction of a musical toy, a moving object or an external noise such as an aeroplane will catch the baby's attention for a few seconds. In the very early stages, an infant's attention will be affected by the lack of control of their head and other movements as they will not be able to look at the object for long or turn towards a noise. At stage one, therefore, the control of attention is external to the child and at the mercy of the environment. It is easy to link this stage with the sensory motor stage described by Piaget in which an infant's attention is action dependent. There is no separation of a child's thinking from external activities.

Stage 2
At this stage, which develops in the second year of life, attention comes under the control of the child. However, attention is rather fixed and inflexible as the child concentrates on something of interest and cannot easily be distracted by something else. It is difficult for the adult to 'break in'.

Stage 3
Now the attention is beginning to move from the rigidity of Stage 2 and the child's attention can be drawn, by an adult, from one thing to another. However, Reynell and her colleagues described this level of attention as 'single channelled' because there can be attention only to one thing at a time. There can be no division of attention and the child's whole auditory and visual interest must be gained. The control of the attention at this stage is with the adult.

Stage 4
The attention at this stage is under the child's own control although it can still be considered 'single channelled'. The child is able to switch from one thing of interest to another but at any one time is concentrating on one thing only. At this stage it would be possible for an adult to attract a child's attention from a task in order to offer them some help. The child, however, would have to pay complete attention to the intervention before returning to the original focus of attention.

Stage 5

At this stage a child is beginning to be able to take in some directions while engaged in a task, provided that the task and the direction are well within the child's understanding. If the instruction is too difficult, then the child reverts to single channelled attention to one task.

Stage 6

At this stage a child is able to integrate two channels of attention. For example, the child may be looking at something and listening to instructions for carrying out an activity at the same time. Reynell and her colleagues suggest that this is the type of attention control required for a child to learn in a class.

Developing shared attention

It has been suggested (e.g. Baron-Cohen 1996) that it is through shared or joint attention that much of our early learning occurs. Pointing and eye contact or gaze direction by both adult and child combined with language or facial expression support shared attention and help a child make sense of the world. This sharing common attention can lead to the development of shared meaning and then turn-taking. Feuerstein (1976) suggested that through this process of mediation of meaning a confusing world of noise or stimuli could be ordered by the child. Attaching meaning to some stimuli and ignoring others helps the child to make sense of the world. Shared attention underpins successful educational encounters. Its establishment and maintenance are of crucial importance for children with speech and language difficulties.

The following strategies (pp. 61–98) support development in the different areas of language use.

Social stories: a social conventions intervention (pragmatics)

Strategy 1:

Clarity of what is expected

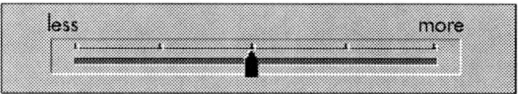

Are the *implicit* learning demands made *explicit* through salient verbal and visual explanation? Does the learner know what the task is and how they have to do it? Does the learner know when the task is finished and what they have to do next? Does the learner know the implicit routines of the school and class? Are areas with specific functions clearly marked? Does the learner know 'the way we do things here' and why? Does the child have a personal timetable so they know where they are in the day and during the week?

Many of the visual strategies described in the section on modality will be useful here.

One method of communicating the implicit social conventions in everyday interaction is through social stories. Developed by Carol Gray (1997) these are not parables about good behaviour but are short, personalised stories created with children to provide them with relevant knowledge and a little background information which help them to understand what is required in social situations. Social stories explain most of the 'hows' and some of the 'whys' of a social interaction. Some children lack the common understandings behind social interaction. They may not have pragmatic skills of communication or if they have they may not be able to judge correctly when they are appropriate.

It is important that the story provides the pupil with accurate and specific social information. Each story begins with detailed information about the situation that the child is finding difficult. This requires careful observation of the target situation in order to gather as many details as possible. This includes the location, who is involved, the nature of the difficulty and what actually happens.

As well as noting observable information it is important to consider possible changes in the situation or routine. For example PE may be timetabled for the same time on the same day each week but it may need to be changed occasionally. The sentence 'PE is usually at 11 o'clock on Wednesday' is therefore a more accurate statement to include in a story than 'PE is at 11 o'clock on Wednesday'. It is also important to ask questions about the target situation, in order to identify aspects that may change.

The pupil may also be able to discuss the situation and provide valuable information. Observation may provide an understanding of the child's perspective. It is this viewpoint that may determine the focus of the social story. It is important to remember, when writing a story, that there are often two valid but different perspectives – that of the adult and that of the child. In order to provide accurate information that is useful to the child, it is important to try to understand the child's perceptions and feelings.

Social stories are usually written in the first person, as though the pupil is describing the event, and Gray (1994) suggests that they should contain three types of sentence: descriptive, perspective and directive. These three types of sentence aim to help the pupil understand the social situation, the perspective of other people and how they should respond.

Descriptive sentences describe what happens, where the situation occurs, who is involved, what they are doing and why. Descriptive sentences are often used to set the scene at the beginning of a story. They should be as accurate as possible and include terms such as 'usually' or 'sometimes' rather than 'always' in order to avoid literal interpretation and help the pupil to cope with possible changes.

Perspective sentences describe the reactions and responses of others in the target situation and sometimes the reasons for those responses. They may also describe the feelings of others.

Directive sentences describe the desired response to the social situation. They tell the child, in positive terms, what he or she should try to do or say in the target situation. As some children with semantic language difficulties often interpret language literally it is important to avoid statements that are inflexible.

It is preferable to use terms such as 'I will try to...' rather than 'I can' or 'I will...', which require absolute compliance.

Carol Gray has developed a ratio which defines the proportions of these sentences. She suggests (but on what basis we are not sure) that there should be a ratio of between two and five descriptive and perspective sentences to every directive sentence in each story, although directive sentences may not always be necessary.

She recommends that this formula is followed regardless of the length of the story. This formula ensures that the pupil is provided with enough detailed information about the target situation so that the story does not end up as just a list of things to do. It is important that the information is meaningful to the child and relevant to their experiences.

The following is an account of a social story created by Carol Rowe with a young boy with Asperger Syndrome who had difficulty coping at lunchtime.

Pupil observation

The pupil was observed in the situation and detailed notes were made in order to obtain a complete picture of the interaction of factors and events.

Direct observation of the situation supported the comments from the school staff. Sean and his support assistant went out onto the playground, with his peers, until it was his class's turn to go into the hall for lunch. He began to complain that he did not want to eat with the other children as he approached the cloakroom to collect his lunch box. His protests became louder as his support assistant tried to encourage and reason with him, he refused to pick up his lunch box and he struggled as she tried to hold his hand. He shouted that the other children were all disgusting because they ate with their mouths open and that they were too noisy. He continued to shout and struggle on his way to the hall. Sean's support assistant was unable to persuade him to enter the hall and he ate his lunch, with his support assistant, away from the other children.

Pupil interview

The pupil was interviewed and his perceptions of the target situation were recorded. During the afternoon of that same day, lunchtime was discussed with Sean. As he enjoys drawing, Sean was asked to draw a picture of lunchtime. We talked about the target situation as he drew. He said that he did not want to eat with the other children as they were 'disgusting because they eat with their mouths open and it's very noisy'. He then drew a picture of himself sitting at a bench in the dining hall with invisible pets (dogs, cats and hamsters) who were all 'eating nicely and not showing me their food'. He drew a speech bubble from his mouth saying, 'This is a nice lunchtime when it is nice and quiet'. It was the pupil's perspective that was to influence the focus of the social story.

Implementation

The story was presented to Sean as a three page book. The support teacher visited the school just before lunch and asked Sean if he remembered drawing me a picture and talking about lunchtime. He said that he did and without prompting once again voiced his concerns about the noise level and the sight of food in the other children's mouths. It was explained that a story had been written to help him at lunchtime. Sean was very enthusiastic when he saw the book and as the story was read to him he made several relevant comments relating to the text.

When we had shared the story his comment was, 'Now I'll know what to do'.

The learning support assistant was asked to continue the use of the story with the pupil. After the initial reading of the story Sean showed the book to his support assistant and they read the story together before going out to the playground before lunch. All other factors in the situation remained constant. The support assistant was asked to refer to the story if, or when, Sean found the situation difficult.

The immediate change in Sean's behaviour was then quite remarkable. During this observation it was noted that he collected his lunch box when asked, walked to the hall with his support assistant, sat at the end of a table and ate his lunch. His behaviour was so settled that his support assistant successfully left him, for a few minutes, while she made herself a cup of coffee. When later asked about this lunchtime Sean responded, 'I've had a happy lunchtime'.

The reading of the story was very gradually reduced after six weeks of daily reading and by the end of the twelve week period the story was no longer read. Although Sean no longer read the story it remained available if he needed to do so. His behaviour continued to be appropriate when the reading of the story ceased and his behaviour at lunchtime was no longer a cause for concern. On the final visit Sean was asked about lunchtimes and he said that they were still happy and commented, 'I don't even read the story, I just remember it'.

There is still a need to establish criteria for the effective application of social stories. It may be that the production of a successful social story is dependent upon the learner realising that there is a problem, followed by the joint generation of possible strategies for the story which are acceptable and possible for the learner (see social reviews below). Social stories are not a panacea.

A social story about lunchtime

Before lunch I am usually in the playground.

A dinner lady tells me when it is time to go and have lunch.

I get my lunch box and then I walk to the hall.

When I go into the hall for lunch there are lots of people there.

Usually it is not just my class.

A grown up usually shows me where to sit.

There are lots of children in the hall who are eating their lunch.

Children often like to talk while they are eating.

There are lots of children in the hall who are talking at the same time.

If the children get too noisy a grown up asks them to talk quietly.

Sometimes children forget to close their mouths when they are eating.

I will try to stay calm and quiet if I see children opening their mouths when they are eating.

I will try to eat my own lunch and not worry about the way the other children are eating their lunch.

Carol Rowe

Self-review of social stories

To what extent does the learner need to have ownership of the story?
   Are the language and concepts used in the social story understood by the learner?
   (Most social stories deal with unstructured time such as lunchtime.)
   Could more be done to structure these times and locations? Why should it be that the most vulnerable child has to do most of the work? Do we need social stories for peers? (Weren't these called good manners in the past?)
   The social story intends to make the implicit demands of a social setting explicit. It possibly provides a new narrative or script for the learner to use. It does provide contextual information for the child to evaluate what is happening.

Strategy 2:

Predictability/novelty

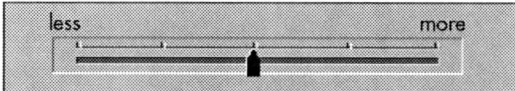

Is the day or lesson structured enough for the child, or is it so structured that it is monotonous and boring? Would different activities, groupings and stimuli vary the novelty of the activities? Is enough happening to keep the child involved or is the child confused by the demands of the task?

The section on visual strategies (p. xx) considers ways of structuring learning tasks and environments.

Strategy 3:

Affirmation/criticism (reward system)

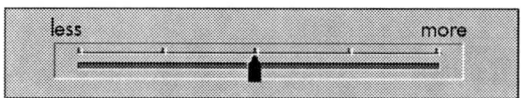

Are there opportunities to reward the real effort of an individual? Does the frequency of the reward need to be increased? Are opportunities for implied or overt negative criticism avoided (e.g. a request for a child to perform their weakest skill in front of an unsympathetic audience of peers)? Are social rewards part of the system? Are the rewards perceived as such by the students? Are rewards administered consistently? Does the learner obtain swift and meaningful feedback about his/her progress?

Strategy 4:

Interaction/group work

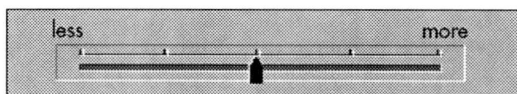

Are flexible groupings in operation which prevent the negative effect of 'bottom set' groups? Are learners able to work by themselves in a quiet area if required, or seek appropriate support from others? Do learners have access to good peer models of social communication?

Peer involvement: Principles

Children with speech and communication difficulties will spend most of their day alongside their peers. Despite this, it is often noted that such children tend to be orientated to adults and may lack friends amongst their peers. This may be because peers may not have the skills in facilitating and repairing conversations as described above or they may be unaware that they need to use them or they may not want to use them. Whether or not these peers also have difficulties in communication, they can provide role models and language opportunities.

Interactions with peers without language and communication difficulties are important as they model language forms and social conventions of interaction which are age appropriate. Peers are a resource. If they do not know how to help they will eventually become a hindrance which may exclude the child with speech and language difficulties.

Peers as gateways to adulthood:

> It has...been argued that communication plays a formative role in the phase known as adolescence. Young people engage in increasingly adult relationships by learning the rules of communication with an ever widening circle of new adults and peers, defining their position in relation to them and gradually moving away from childhood and into adulthood.
>
> (Cazan *et al*. 1996)

An adolescent who does not develop this ever widening circle of acquaintances and therefore does not engage in these important conversations is going to miss out. They are likely not to be party to the cultural world of adolescence.

Did you hear what Grant said to Tiffany?

It may be that characters in TV soaps can also become part of the circle of adults and peers to be gossiped about amongst peers, thus providing role models of attitudes and actions to be aped or abhorred.

Mentors

For older children, the importance of quality conversational interactions with mentors has been noted in a BT survey of effective communication in teenage years:

> Mentors – defined in the survey as 'an older friend who advises you' – play a special role in the lives of young people as they provide a source of advice and support on personal and confidential matters that is independent of the family, more experienced than a peer and possibly easier to approach than a professional adult. No age was specified, so the mentors included by respondents in their communication map could have been another slightly older teenager or an adult with special status for the teenager.
>
> (Cazan *et al*. 1996)

Peers/buddy systems: Institutional self-review

- Are children aware of the difficulties that peers may have with speech and communication?

- Are peers aware of the strengths and unique characteristics that these learners may have, e.g. good memory, determination, sense of humour?

- Are the learners with speech and language difficulties regarded as individuals?

- Do peers know how they can help other children to communicate? If not, has training been given?

- Do peers know how to help other children to join in activities?

- Do peers know when to do so and when not to help?

- Are peers supported in helping an identified child?

OHP 3

Peer involvement: Ideas for action

Peers may need to be taught explicitly:

- awareness of a child's language or communication difficulties;

- empathy with what it must be like to face those difficulties in school and home;

- the range of skills that they can use to help the child (listed below in the section on social skills training);

- when and where they need to use these skills.

This will depend upon the abilities of the peers but can work with even very young children.

Circles of friends (developing empathy and peer support)

This is a peer support strategy developed in North America (Peerpoint *et al.* 1992) to support the inclusion of children with a diversity of special needs. The name for this intervention is based upon the view that many children with special needs will have an outer circle of acquaintances but lack an inner circle of friends. The strategy can link in with circle time and other approaches. Its aim is to establish a support group of peers who will help a child with special needs to be included within the life of the school.

Taylor (1997) describes the process, as follows.

1. Establishing prerequisites, which involves selecting a school with a suitably supportive ethos and negotiating the necessary commitment of resources (typically 30–40 minutes of teacher time weekly to facilitate a meeting involving six to eight students). The parents and focus child are then approached.

2. A discussion with the class or tutor group, which is usually undertaken by an outsider, focuses on the child's strengths and difficulties and invites class members to empathise with him or her and to build on his or her own experience of friendships.

3. Establishing a circle. A representative group of six to eight volunteers meets with the focus child and an adult facilitator. The class discussion is summarised, a collaborative approach to problem solving is established and practical arrangements are determined.

4. Weekly meetings of the 'circle'. The children and the member of the school staff meet weekly to review progress, identify difficulties and plan practical steps to solve them.

Those kids were certainly not bad for a bunch of amateurs!

Whitaker *et al.* (1998) have trialled the approach in this country for learners with autism. They note that while true friendships with the focus child did not develop, an increase in play with same aged peers was reported, coupled with decreased anxiety. The circle volunteers reported that they would be willing to do it again if asked. As overt training in ways to deal with social/communication problems was not explicitly included these approaches look quite promising.

Buddy/mentor systems

Gill Moorcroft (1998) suggests the following ways of encouraging peer support.

1. Talk to the student's classmates/year group about speech and communication difficulties in positive terms. This may need to be repeated.

2. Explain some of the more obvious difficulties that the student may have.

3. Establish a group of friends – coming to school, break times, lunchtimes, after-school activities. Friendships, though, will need time to develop naturally.

4. Arrange a buddy system.

5. Use the student's strengths and interests to enable him/her to help peers.

6. Set up opportunities for sharing, e.g. computer, board games, etc.

7. Encourage class mates to work alongside him/her if the student is still comparatively isolated.

8. Answer all questions about the student's difficulties with honesty and in a positive light.

9. Most children do want friends – being alone may be easier for them, but they can be lonely.

10. Bullying can be a problem if peer support is not in place.

11. The student with speech and communication difficulties needs peer support but the peers need support as well.

12. Peer support needs to be encouraged, nurtured and monitored.

> Peer support needs the support of regular meetings with a member of staff so that they can inform and be informed by the targets in the IEP.

Circle time can be used to support the maintenance and generalisation of social skills developed through peer support and is discussed below.

Random pairs

Within a classroom a variety of sub-groups can develop, which means that opportunities for the direct modelling and development of language and social skills may be restricted.

Randomly pairing children within the class can overcome this. McNamara and Moreton (1995) suggest starting with simple social interactions of a short duration to begin with and then increasing the complexity and duration. This can form part of circle time activities after children have been randomised by a 'swap places if...' activity.

'Swap places if your favourite colour is green.'
'Swap places if you like toffee.'
'Swap places if you have brown hair.'
'Swap places if you are wearing something with red on it.'

Volunteer help

The elderly as mentors
A number of projects have utilised the involvement of the elderly in schools, especially when there is a community school ethos. This has taken a variety of forms:

- the elderly being involved in reminiscence activities where the child seeks information about local history from local photographs and artefacts;

- the elderly engaged with the learner in a game or task.

Sixth formers and work placement

In a similar way older pupils or students may be able to be programmed in as part of a course option over a number of weeks or preferably over the year. The students will need the awareness and social skills development training described above.

Reverse integration
Units and special schools frequently invite in children from the mainstream to share their facilities with children who attend the school or unit to provide opportunities for socialisation. The term 'reverse integration' is really a poor term as it logically implies segregation, which is obviously not the intended goal. Thankfully, a name describing the activities is often used instead, e.g. Computer Club, Snack Club, or Games Club.

Circle time

Circle time is a flexible framework that can be used to meet a wide range of targets. It is a structured set of turn-taking activities which occur with learners usually seated on chairs of the same height in a circle with the teacher. It has starting, middle and ending activities. Typical activities include the following.

- Sentence completion

'My name is...'

'I am good at...'

'I like to have friends because...'

'I find it easiest to work in class when...'

'Well done to _____ because _____'

'Would it be helpful if...'

During a talking activity, a speaking object is passed around. This can be a conch, a pretend microphone, a soft toy, an alabaster egg or any agreed object. No one may speak unless they are holding the speaking object.

- Actions

Passing a smile round the circle.
A child says a feeling and the circle make an appropriate face to indicate that feeling.
All change where a category is called out and all children who fit that category change places, e.g. has black hair, has a pet...
Passing clapping – a clap is passed round the circle.
Clap back – as above but the direction of clapping changes when a child claps twice quickly.

> Circle Time has recently become a 'buzz' term in education, and like any new trend, it is really vulnerable to misuse and abuse. I have heard it applied equally to a superficial newsround where children shouted out one word responses and to a worryingly intense discussion amongst pupils about an absent peer; in both cases the teachers had failed to adhere to the basic Circle-Time ground-rules or structures I advocate and to understand fully its true potential as a forum for individual and organisational change.
>
> (Mosley 1996)

Behind circle time is a set of principles, attitudes and skills which the teacher is encouraged to adopt and develop within children. Some of these are stated explicitly in the form of golden rules, which are also available in poster format from LDA and are intended to be applicable throughout the school day.

Do be gentle	– Don't hurt anybody
Do be kind and helpful	– Don't hurt people's feelings
Do listen	– Don't interrupt
Do work hard	– Don't waste your or other people's time
Do look after property	– Don't waste or damage it
Do be honest	– Don't cover up the truth

Much as we'd hate to break one of the golden rules (we want to be helpful but it might hurt people's feelings), circle time has a lot of personal growth verbalising which may go beyond the understanding of many children with speech and language difficulties. They may need prioritising and explanation visually, with photos, and through physical examples.

Children who have semantic difficulties may take these rules literally if they are not mixed and paired.

'Do be honest' is not a recommendation to comment on the size of staff and helpers' bottoms or another child's facial disfigurement because you 'Don't hurt people's feelings' and ' "Yes we know it says "Don't cover up the truth". These "golden rules" may need platinum exceptions'.

'Don't waste your or other people's time' may be interpreted by a child as a licence to avoid the faltering attempts at communication from a child with speech and language difficulties if not countered with the rule 'Do listen'.

Circle time is a valuable framework if it is applied flexibly. As always, it is only as good as the teacher that applies it. It is a means not the end.

Circle time: Self-review

Are the tasks/games at the appropriate level to be understood by the members of the circle? That is:

- Do the members of the circle have the necessary social skills (refer to social skills model above)?

- Are the members of the circle able to understand the tasks set?

- Are the members of the circle able to use the language required for the tasks?

If not then games should be modified to develop the required skills.

Is the circle time valued as an important and relevant activity by those involved?

Is circle time an end in itself or another educational tool that can meet a number of aims?

Are there enough positive role models in the group (either peers or adults) to demonstrate the appropriate skills required?

Circle time: Ideas for action

Many activities for developing language skills and turn-taking can occur in a circle time format while meeting other curriculum goals.

Goldthorpe (1998) suggests that the following skills are needed for circle time:

good listening;
good speaking (which involves knowing when not to speak);
looking skills;
good thinking;
good concentrating.

If these are taken for granted by the teacher or the circle then the child who does not have these skills will fail. However, they are explicit skills which can be taught and developed within a circle time framework and are key social skills for all children.

We note a number of occasions where children with speech and communication difficulties have been excluded because their main problem was that 'they could not cope with circle time'. Anyone who needs instructions for this process can do no better than refer to Mosley's chapter on 'Children Beyond' in her book *Quality Circle Time in the Primary School*. In her terms:

'A Child Beyond' is one who has been offered, yet failed to respond to regular, empathetic listening opportunities, participation in Circle Time, promotion of the Golden Rules, regular incentives to help him uphold these and the safe boundaries of a sanctions system based upon the withdrawing of privileges that he has identified as valuable. Despite all these measures, the child continues to adhere to disruptive or unhappy behaviour.

(Mosley 1996, p. 50)

Mosley does warn against applying the term too easily to a child whose problems really arise from a cycle of negative interactions with peers, and notes that many vulnerable children can be frequently and surreptitiously set up and wound up by peers so that they are always in trouble with the teacher.

Mosley's solution to the 'child beyond' is to remove him or her to a school based therapeutic circle group or referral to play therapy. Pearcey (1996) suggests that 'Circle Time works...because it is grounded in sound psychology'.

It fails, however, when this psychology is wrongly applied. The psychology Pearcey refers to includes the therapeutic approaches of Carl Rogers and the symbolic interactions theory of G. H. Mead. The latter suggests that:

The first stage of the individual self is constituted simply by an organisation of the particular attitudes of other individuals towards himself...but at the second stage...also by an organisation of the social attitudes of the generalised other or the social group as a whole to which he belongs.

(Mead 1934)

This presumes a good grounding in knowledge of other people. It produces an awareness that they have beliefs and attitudes which they convey through their verbal and non-verbal behaviour to us. Their attitudes towards and about us can be used to help us form our identities. Mead is not wrong. He is in fact predicting – 62 years previously – the BT study results (Cazan *et al.* 1996) cited above. The problem is that the inability to obtain this information or make use of it within a circle leads to the child being labelled as 'beyond' or 'disturbed'.

> One of the authors of this book provides an account of when he first came to Kent and wandered from the bar into the garden of the pub on a summer's evening. In the garden the local branch of the Esperanto Society were diligently practising their language around the traditional Kentish pub game of bat and trap. On being recognised by a colleague he was encouraged to join in, in Esperanto. He had no knowledge of the game or the language.
>
> Was he disturbed?   Yes.
> Was he a 'man beyond'?   For a time, he wished he was.

Failure in circle time should not lead to the attribution of 'mad', 'sad' or 'bad' labels automatically. The child may have language or communication difficulties and may just not understand what is required.

Fortunately, such a child is not 'beyond' the Code of Practice so that the stages of identifying concerns, agreeing targets and reviewing progress with colleagues may mean that the child's needs become more important than those of the circle.

> 'Sometimes the hippies have to take their baggage off the bus because it is just getting too heavy.'
>
> Punk slogan from the seventies

Circle time can be a tool for meeting the needs of children with speech and language difficulties by focusing upon the development of the skills outlined above through a wide range of games and activities (see the resource list). It can also be an opportunity to set targets and review the application of those skills in other settings during the week.

Goldthorpe (1998) has shown that circle time can provide a framework for peer support within IEPs. The following is an adaptation of her framework to include roles for peers.

Goldthorpe's framework for incorporating IEPs within circle time

Goldthorpe notes that children in the circle may come up with negative comments which nevertheless may need to be addressed in a positive manner referring to the golden rules. There is a danger that negative and superficial targets may arise as a result of the perception of a child's behaviour being the central problem rather than their lack of understanding or social skills.

Why	Why are we worried about them?	Concerns	Circle time to discuss child's problem sensitively, directly or indirectly. Concern may arise during circle time, e.g. from a game. 'I feel happy at lunchtimes when...' 'I feel unhappy at lunch times when...'
Where	Where do we want them to be?	Aims	Golden rules will provide a framework.
What	What do we want them to do?	Targets	Select achievable targets which may arise from circle time.
How	How are we going to get there?	Strategies	Circle time can provide many of these via 'Would it help if...?' type games.
Who	Who is going to help?	Roles	Circle time could elicit volunteers or identify other people who could be called upon for help via 'I could help by...'.
When	When are we going to see if they are getting there? Date.	Review	Circle time may be used for this. Perhaps a staff circle?

Some guidelines for circle time

1. There are two basic assumptions:
    (a) everyone is a valuable member of the group;
    (b) every group is capable of working together.
2. There are three simple rules:
    (a) take turns to speak;
    (b) listen to each other;
    (c) have fun without spoiling anyone else's fun.

WHEN and WHERE
1. *Primary:* if room size is a problem add circle time on to a music or story session where children are already away from their tables, or move the furniture during break.
2. *Secondary:*
    (a) use PSE, drama, form tutor time or break time;
    (b) sessions should be regular and given status;
    (c) limit the time, infants – 10 minutes, juniors and secondary – 20/40 minutes.

HOW
1. Sit in a circle with an agreed leader.
2. Everyone should sit at the same level if possible.

3. Set the rules, which are basically *good listening skills*.
4. The rules are for *all* to follow, including the group leader. They should outline behaviours that show respect and caring towards oneself, one another and all property.
5. Rules which can become part of the circle time ideal may be as follows:

    - take turns to speak – listen to each other (a 'talking' object can be used);
    - be kind and respectful – no one makes comments which are judgements, put downs or critical or hurtful remarks (not even as a response to 'inappropriate' responses);
    - you may 'pass' in a round – but then must sit quietly;
    - don't name names – you can talk about a problem, e.g. being bullied, but never name the bully.

6. Strategies may be needed for those who *choose* not to keep the rules.
7. Ensure an overall positive feeling.
8. Praise good listening, etc.
9. Circle time should begin and end with enjoyable routines.
10. The idea of confidentiality should be promoted. Encourage pupils to say only what they feel safe with. (This may be difficult for young children or children with speech and language difficulties, who may not have sophisticated notions of conversational appropriateness.)

PLANNING
1. Plan the session but be prepared to be flexible.
2. Keep the activities varied.
3. Help the shy pupil by sharing ideas for the 'round' before the session and make the activities non-threatening.
4. The session focus can take into account the current concerns or anxieties.
5. It can be used to address problems and to find acceptable solutions.
6. Aim for a balance of personalities and needs within a group.
7. Always evaluate for yourself and sometimes with the pupils.

(Ashford Learning Support Service Team, Kent County Council)

Social skills: Principles

Social skills training (pragmatics)

Spence (1977) suggests that social skills are 'those components of social behaviour which are necessary to ensure that individuals achieve their desired outcome from a social interaction...or...appropriate social behaviour within a particular social situation'.

Kelly (1996) groups social skills in the following way:

Social skills			
Non-verbal behaviour		**Verbal behaviour**	**Assertiveness behaviour**
Body language	*Paralinguistic Skills (vocal cues)*		
Eye contact	Volume	Listening	Expressing feelings
Facial expression	Rate or speed	Opening a conversation	Standing up for yourself
Gesture	Clarity	Taking turns	Making suggestions
Proximity	Intonation (prosody)	Asking questions	Refusing
Touch	Fluency	Answering questions	Disagreeing
Fidgeting		Relevancy	Complaining
Posture		Repair	Apologising
Personal appearance		Ending a conversation	Requesting explanations

Social skills: Ideas for action

These skills can be taught explicitly in a variety of settings and groups through explicit modelling and imitation activities. Self-awareness and self-monitoring in the development of social skills have been noted as important indicators of the success of social skills training programmes. Both *Talkabout* (Kelly 1996) and the *Social Use of Language Programme* (Rinaldi 1992) are examples of social skills programmes which include self-assessment and self-awareness elements. Speech and language therapists and specialist advisory teachers in speech and language sometimes will help set up social skills groups in schools which are then operated by learning support assistants.

Hundert (1995) suggests criteria for such programmes, as follows.

Positive

Learning how to think in a variety of real social situations using a number of applied strategies rather than scripted solutions to specific problems.

Consistent

In presentation with skills modelled by a teacher or facilitator with visual support and critical analysis of component skills. In membership and location with staff and parents aware of goals and strategies so that they are applied across settings.

Visual

Consistent visuals using line drawings to depict the skills with a standard layout. These visuals may need to be displayed where the skill is to be applied.

Flexible

So that they can be modified to meet the needs of teachers and students and the school setting.

Manageable

The programmes should be possible within the available resources of time, personnel and specialist input.

Supportive

The programmes should contribute to the curriculum delivery within schools and be applicable within many of the existing activities ongoing throughout the school day.

Developing social skills

The approach should include the following.

1. *Modelling*: viewing the modelling teaches the pupil what to do.
2. *Role play*: its use gives the pupils practice in how to do it.
3. *Performance feedback*: information on how well they have done and its effect. This can teach pupils why they should behave in certain ways.
4. *Transfer*: opportunities to practise the skills needed to be built into the programme. This should involve school and home. Positive reinforcement and encouragement are essential.

Social skills development can support:

- whole-school approaches to behaviour;

- personal and social education;

- the development of that most elusive construct, self-esteem (frequently found to be lacking in learners but rarely operationally defined).

The activities described in social skills programmes can readily be applied to circle time groups, which may include peers and mentors.

Social skills: Institutional self-review

Social review

Digital video cameras with high quality playback and stills are a very rare resource in schools but may have a great potential for developing self-awareness of social skills. This is termed 'social review' by Carol Gray (1995), who attempted to assess informally the understanding and perceptions of a videotaped social situation by a learner who is able to communicate verbally or with a communication aid. In social review, the teacher describes objectively what is happening, and then the learner's viewpoint of what is happening is solicited and explored. Bieber (1994) refers to the exploration of social mistakes as social autopsies where the learner engages in a discussion with an adult of what went wrong, the aim being to develop a plan to overcome the problem which may be written down or depicted in symbols or pictures.

This appears to be very similar to the social story technique described in this book. Attwood (1998) has done similar work using the TV series 'Third Rock From The Sun' and 'Mr Bean', whose central characters tend towards misunderstanding social situations *'with hilarious consequences for all involved'*.

The success of social review is clearly dependent upon a learner's understanding of social skills and should be seen as part of social skills training.

Teachable moments or incidental teaching

These help to generalise or support social skill development (Adams 1997). They include:

- praise for the use of appropriate language and conversational skills when they occur in everyday use; the praise should state exactly what the learner is doing right;

- stating when the learner is not doing something correctly and why.

Perhaps refer to a visual prompt, i.e. a poster showing 'good listening';

- invite the learner to try again;

- use prompting and cueing,
  e.g. *'John, Peter has just come over to us. He has a bag of crisps in his hand. I think he wants to ask you something...'* ;

- commenting on an aspect of social interaction that the learner has missed:
  'John, Mary is looking away from you'.

Adult interventions to help develop language and communication: semantics and pragmatic language

Parental involvement

When an adult converses with a child they frequently adapt the way they communicate to accommodate the language skills and understanding of the child. For example, the adult's sentences are simplified whereas the child's phrases may be repeated back to the child in elaborated form. The adult may slow down his usual speech rate, use simpler words and exaggerate stress and intonation. Adults do this without thinking because it is part of our nature. However, these strategies to encourage conversation and understanding may be underused in education, where they are especially important for learners with speech and communication difficulties.

> Children are typically engaged when they are motivated and understand the meaning and purpose of the social dynamic (a conversation, or shared event or activity). When a child does not understand the meaning behind messages and events in the situation, the activity needs to be clarified and/or simplified.
>
> (Quill 1997)

Adult interventions: Ideas for action

Margery Rappaport (1996) suggests the following approaches for language development with the pre-verbal child, the child beginning to use words and the child using creative multi-word utterances.

1. *Minimise direct questions*

Adults often think that language and communication can be developed by asking lots of 'Wh' questions of the type:

What is this?
Where are you going?
What are you doing?
What do you call this?

Quill (1997) notes:

> There is a tendency for adults to control interactions with language-impaired children through language that focuses the child's attention then asks questions or commands

the child to do something. Given that the purpose of conversation is to share information, it is important to use language that focuses on what is happening at the moment.

Although you can't and won't want to eliminate these questions entirely, they are overused at the expense of the following alternative strategies.

2. *Commenting*
Follow the child's lead, watch what he or she is doing and then comment upon it. Provide a narrative of what is happening that might represent the child's own internal dialogue. Comment upon your own parallel actions. For a more able child you may want to include interpretations of feelings and thoughts, intent and perspective (Quill).

3. *Wait and signal in a communicative exchange*
After an adult has spoken he or she waits and communicates non-verbally that a response is expected from the child by looking expectantly, that is, with eye contact established, lips are moved slightly apart, eyebrows are raised and the head and body are oriented towards the child.

Some children with autism do find eye contact physically painful (as noted by Grandin (1995) and Williams (1997)) and may also object to the intrusion on their personal space, in which case joint attention can be focused upon some common object or visual prompt (see the section on visual strategies).

4. *Set up communicative situations*
This can be done by avoiding the anticipation of the child's every need and being on the look out for conversational opportunities in everyday events. The learner then has to communicate to get what they want. For example, put the child's favourite videos or toys out of reach but in view so the child has to point or use a name to get what they want.

Give them their usual breakfast but miss out a vital element then look expectantly at them!

For example, put out the cereal without the spoon.

5. *Use abundant gesture and facial expression*
Exaggerate your tone of voice and facial expression to get the message across. However, be wary of the child's ability to mimic without understanding so that the child's communication becomes theatrical and inappropriate.

For example:

'Look, the ketchup bottle top is stuck!'
Exaggerated twisting of bottle top with suitable facial contortions.
'It is stuck!'

6. *Modelling*
Rather than correcting mistakes appropriate phrases and sentences are suggested for the learner. This helps you to focus on what the child is trying to communicate rather than how she is communicating.

7. *Reduction*
Early years teachers were sometimes exhorted to 'bathe the child in language' by using lots of spoken language. Unfortunately, this indiscriminate use of a cheap resource meant that many children with speech and language difficulties ended up confused and frustrated. They were not bathing, they were drowning! When commenting, responding

or modelling language simplify what you say. Reduce the complexity to increase the clarity of what you mean so that it is at the level of the child. For example, if the child is not yet speaking then speak in one word utterances as much as possible.

Hodgon (1995) suggests that reducing the amount of language used with learners with speech and language difficulties will reduce the complexity of their auditory environment. She suggests the reduction of language to key phrases which are simple but grammatical and then pairing them with visual prompts (see below) when appropriate.

For example,
'Sit on the carpet'
becomes
'Sit';

'Go to the cloakroom and get your lunch box'
becomes
'Get your lunch'.

It may be tempting to use telegraphic or 'pidgin' English but the purpose is to model the reduction of language that developmentally typical children may use.

8. *Use exaggerated intonation, volume and rate of speech*
This will help the learner to attend to what is being said and is why songs and nursery rhymes are so often used for stimulating early language development – because they are repetitive and rhythmical. However, some children will respond best to a voice that is calm, slow and highly predictable.

9. *Eye contact and direction of gaze*
For more accomplished communicators, the use of gaze can help us to take it in turns in conversation and to establish joint attention. As stated above, forced eye contact may be extremely uncomfortable for some children, so hectoring commands such as 'look at me' from an adult may not encourage the child to use eye contact and gaze appropriately. For example, the child who mechanically looks someone straight in the eye when engaged in conversation is likely to get into trouble very quickly. 'Establishing joint attention on an object or action is more important than maintaining a vacuous eye gaze' (Quill).

There is nothing to stop you moving your head close to the action or object or the other way round so that eye contact occurs 'naturally'.

10. *Reinforcement or responsiveness*
Do not ignore attempts to communicate, whatever form they take. They may be verbal or non-verbal.

A response will increase the child's efforts to communicate.

Jordan and Powell (1996) suggest that an adult may wish consistently to give meaning to a learner's utterance or action despite being uncertain that the learner has a communicative intention. For example, the adult might regularly interpret a specific utterance by a person with severe communication difficulties as wanting to leave the room. 'Oh, Rajik wants to leave the room.' This attribution of meaning to a regular utterance may then come to be understood by the learner.

Unconventional or challenging means of communication can be changed into more conventional means. For example, a child who does a drawing and then tears it up when they have finished may need to be taught an alternative way of finishing...perhaps by putting the drawing into a 'finished' tray which may have a symbol on it.

Rappaport's eleventh recommendation is to make it fun. This is clearly part of reinforcement, so here it is not treated as a separate section. Clearly, if communication and language are to develop they need to be fun. Rather than being clinical they should be relaxed and playful. The more the child enjoys being engaged in meaningful communication, the more he or she will seek it out.

Theo Peeters (1997) considers the role of others in dealing with people with social communication difficulties that are often found in autism. He suggests that as people without social and communication difficulties are more flexible than those who have them, it is a simple 'moral politeness' to be flexible in order to communicate with them. The more flexible mind helps the less flexible one.

More than ten years before the National Curriculum and 15 years before the Code of Practice, when inclusion and differentiation did not have the meanings they have now, Joan Tough was providing advice for teachers and parents about how they could help learners with language difficulties.

Between adults who use language effectively, there can still be wide gaps in meanings, misunderstandings can and often do, take place. But when the child and the adult talk there is likely to be a wider gulf between their meanings. This gap can only be reduced by the adult who can try to understand the child's view, to get inside him as it were, and see his problems. The adult who understands what the child's problems in communication are is able to help the child by trying to give him the motivation he needs for expressing his ideas, and for helping him to appreciate the kind of information that the listener needs to be given, as well as helping the child to project into the adult's intentions and meanings as he listens to the adult's talk. What the adult expresses, and the way in which he expresses his meaning, must take account of the child's difficulties.

It is through the experiences gained with adults who take up a tutorial relationship with him that the child is gradually able to gain insight into others' perspectives. In this relation-ship the child is continually helped to reflect on what he knows, to reconsider what he has said, to give attention to the essential elements of his experiences and try to put them into a structure. The child needs continual encouragement to make an internal inspection of his own experiences and ideas. The child also needs help if he is to project beyond him-self and his own experiences. The tutoring adult helps by indicating the problems he has in understanding the child, giving the child clues on what further information is needed and thus helping the child to build up strategies that are effective for communication.

It is the continual alternation in dialogue between the inspection of one's own meanings and considering the problems of communication that seems to provide not only the basis from which the child will build knowledge of language and the skills of communication but also the means of becoming reflective.

(Tough 1977)

Since then language development has been relegated within the curriculum to the service role of speaking and listening to support the development of literacy. What once was a central role for the teacher in some schools has moved to the periphery of classroom practice. Teachers may have become de-skilled in language development to the extent that it frequently has to be delegated to others due to the dictates of the one true resource – that is, time.

Strategy 5:

Available time for tasks (workload)

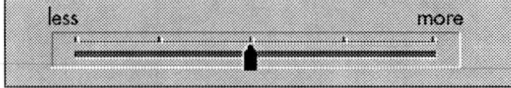

Is the workload appropriate for the learner? Has she too much or too little to do? Is the amount of time available for tasks, including homework, enough? Could the learner increase their work rate via the use of a laptop, computer or amanuensis?

Waiting for a response is important for a child with communication difficulties. They may need more time to organise a response due to processing difficulties which may occur at different levels. For example they may have difficulty attributing the appropriate meaning to what they have seen and heard or they may need time to select and then generate an appropriate response.

Strategy 6:

Negotiation/conflict (choice)

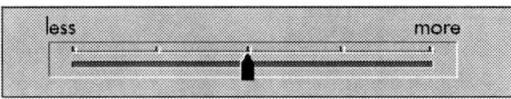

Does the learner have choice? Is she supported to develop independent learning and social skills? Are there opportunities for 'real' negotiation so that serious conflict can be avoided ? Is there a flexible and fair system of negotiation available for all learners? Is the child totally dependent and not given choices? In the context of speech and language difficulties, does he or she have the necessary skills to make a request or choose from or negotiate alternatives?

Strategy 7:

Level of tasks (complexity)

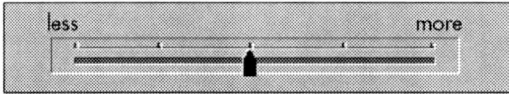

Is the work easy enough for the learner to do? Could it be broken down into smaller constituent tasks? On the other hand, does it set enough challenges? Are links made with other areas?

Strategy 8:

Modality

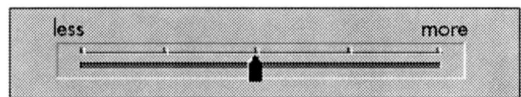

Are tasks set, undertaken and presented just using spoken language? Can sensory approaches be applied so that the preferred modality of the learner is emphasised? Can the learner be taught to make better use of a modality of instruction?

Auditory discrimination (phonological/morphological)

Development of listening

- How Do I Sound game – sentences are written on cards which will be used to demonstrate appropriate changes in volume of speech, e.g. 'Don't wake the baby', 'Isn't this lecture boring!', 'Could everybody please stop talking and listen for a moment.'

- The Bear And The Honeypot game – one child is blindfolded and sits in the middle of the circle with a box or pot representing honey next to him/her. The teacher points to a child, who tries to take the honeypot from the bear. The bear should listen carefully and point to the person creeping up on them.

- Ask the child if the words are same or different, e.g. rug–bug – which word does not belong? Give the child a list of words that have the same beginning sound.

To increase auditory discrimination

- Only auditory – have the child close his eyes so vision does not disturb auditory discrimination.

- By the intensification of auditory stimulus – make the sounds louder, being sure background noise is at a reduced level.

- By visual cues – show the child the visual representation of the auditory stimulus; show the child how the sound is made on the lips, position of the tongue and teeth.

- Kinaesthetically – have the child touch his/her own or the teacher's voice parts. Watching the teacher's lips, feeling his/her and the teacher's voice parts as they work and looking at his/her own production of speech sounds in a mirror will be beneficial.

- Child distinguishes which percussion instrument is being played (having listened to each one first).

- Use sound boxes and ask children to guess the contents.

- Use picture of train with engine, freight car and caboose to sort out CVC words, e.g. middle letter foes in the freight car.

- Play note on instrument. Child indicates when the same note is played again.

- Child listens to a series of sentences and acts out the one that is different.

- Hide a ticking clock. Child finds it by listening out for ticks.

- When teaching letter sounds, identify them with familiar sounds, e.g. 'What sound do you make when you blow out a candle?', 'What sound do you make when you eat something good?'

- Use sound wheels – the child spins a circle and reads the word he has made.

- Listen to recorded sounds and then ask the child to demonstrate the sound, e.g. opening a door.

- Play sound bingo.

- On a list of rhyming words, ask the child to circle the parts of the words that are alike.

- Ladder words
- change the vowel to make a new word, e.g. cat, cut, cot;
- change the beginning consonant;
- change the ending consonant;
- change a letter – give word-fill;
- change one letter and get something we use to grind flour;
- change one letter and get something which is part of a bird, etc.;
- ask the child to make up a riddle whose answer begins with the last letter of the answer to the previous riddle;
- prepare index cards with letter, diphthong blends, digraphs. When the child hears the sound, he/she holds up the appropriate card;
- using pictures, sort into groups of rhyming words.

- This can be extended to the adult reading a word and the child circling the word he/she hears:
- ask the child to listen to a list of words and tell you how they are alike – use several words beginning with the same letter;
- play a listening game in which the children signal by raising a hand, clapping or standing whenever you pronounce a word which begins with a certain letter;

- give the child four or five words; ask which two words begin with the same sound;
- tape record voices of class peers and ask the child to identify the voices; this can be extended to disguising voices;
- dramatise sounds, e.g. clock ticking;
- select a short story or poem and ask the child to signal for a particular word or sound; this can be extended by the child searching for two or three words/sounds and giving different signals for each;
- read out a silly alliterative sentence; which words do not begin with the given sound?;
- use sound tapes to distinguish sounds;
- clap for words beginning with...;
- look for sounds which are similar;
- find rhyming words.

- Make a rhyming book:
- discriminate between CVC words which have the same middle vowel;
- give the child a word and have him/her give as many words as possible which have the same beginning, middle or ending sound;
- play 'Say It, Take It'. Child extracts objects beginning with a particular sound, from a variety of objects on the table.

To develop auditory memory
Keep commands short and simple:

- Learning rhymes/chants/fun poems.

- Shopping game – as a variant, add objects using each letter of the alphabet.

- Child watches and listens as beads are dropped into a can. The child then has to copy this, dropping the same number into the can – this can be extended – with the child's eyes closed.

- Copying rhythms which are tapped out. Use percussion instruments for variation.

- Re-tell simple stories.

- Give child a series of verbal commands. Start with two and then gradually increase the number.

- Ask the child to finish a pattern of sound, e.g. slish, slosh, slish, ... Percussion instruments can be used here.

- Place card in front of teacher/assistant's mouth (to limit visual cues) – ask child to repeat a series of nonsense syllables, digits, phrases, sentences.

- Clapping simple patterns – child then produces own pattern.

- Use taped story. Ask questions about it, e.g. 'How did the story finish?'

- Play imitation game – teacher/friend carries out a series of sequences which child has to copy, e.g. bounce a ball, snap fingers, cough, etc. This can be recorded and compared with the original.

- Give child a string of words. Ask him/her to remember middle word.

- Play 'I Went On A Trip. In My Suitcase I Put...' – adaptation of shopping game.

- Child closes eyes and concentrates for 30 seconds or more. What sounds can he/she hear? Where do they come from?

- Give the child a list of nonsense syllables. Repeat the list leaving out one syllable. Can the child identify that syllable?

- Ask the child to listen to TV/radio daily for specific information, e.g. weather, sports scores. Report findings to class.

- Restaurant game. One child plays the waiter and must remember the orders to be given to the cook.

- Memorise number sequence – forwards then backwards.

- Read off a series of symbols, numbers, letters, words that contain two or more of the same symbols. The child selects the duplications.

- Read a story. Then read several sentences and ask whether the child remembers hearing them in the story just read.

- Number Series game, e.g. 'Listen to these numbers and say the one in the series that is closest to...'

- Ask the child to alphabetise a series of three or four words presented orally.

- Each child is assigned a word. The teacher reads a story. Every time the child's word is mentioned, he/she raises hand.

- Read aloud the names of different objects, including three or four different categories. Ask the child to concentrate on and remember one word from one category only.

- Read a sentence to the child which he/she repeats verbatim. Then read the sentence omitting a word. Child provides missing word.

- Ask the child to reproduce a series of movements presented orally, e.g. hop, hop, skip.

- Play 'First Letter Only' game – the first letter of each word spells out a word.

- Give the child a series of numbers/letters. Ask questions about them, e.g. 'What the first/last number/letter?', 'What number/letter came before...?'

- Use mnemonic devices for remembering, e.g. E G B D F = Every Good Boy Deserves Food.

- Ask the child to re-arrange sentences verbally, e.g. 'the ran boy'.

- Ask the child to repeat instructions before initiating action.

- Use nonsense phrases or sentences for oral and written work, e.g. 'happy hippopotami hibernate hevery holiday'.

- Increase sentences, e.g. 'I see:
  I see a cat
  I see a black cat.

- Present the same words over and over until internalised, but using the words in a variety of contexts.

- Programme materials so that new items build on previously learned material.

- Limit vocabulary that is meaningless to the child.

- Make vocabulary meaningful by planned repetition of those words that are essential for the child to learn.

- Use visual cues to support auditory stimuli.

To increase auditory perception

- Blindfold child. Ask him/her to point in direction from which adult is speaking. Move around after each time.

- Ask child to point to direction of sound.

- Play tape of various sounds. Ask child to describe what is happening.

To develop auditory–vocal association

- Ask one-concept questions.

- Provide visual clues wherever possible to reinforce the spoken word.

- Give ample time for responses.

- Give the child a written question to think about before calling upon him/her to answer orally.

- Use short sentences and simple directions.

- Permit short answers from the child.

- Teach through concrete objects before attempting abstractions.

- Develop the child's responsiveness by having him/her imitate simple actions.

- Play the game 'Charades'.

- Ask questions using multiple choice answers, e.g. 'Do we draw with a pencil or scissors?'

- Use riddles, e.g. 'I am an animal and I have a long trunk'.

- Extend this by giving the child a picture and asking him/her to write own riddle.

- Child wears animal picture on forehead, for example. He/she asks questions about the animals to gain more information about the one he/she is wearing.

- Ask child which word would be appropriate for completion of sentence, e.g. 'I can sleep on a...' (banana, bed, bike).

- Select word which is odd one out of certain categories.

- Ask questions which require a 'yes' or 'no' answer, e.g. 'If you walk on dry leaves would you hear a sound?'

- Ask the child to predict the outcome of short stories. Give a selection of endings (including inappropriate ones) if necessary.

- Describe an object or picture in terms of its characteristics, functions and uses, and ask the child to decide which object/picture was being described.

- Use classification games, discussing each item as it is identified as to why it is being placed in each category.

- Use word associations, e.g. 'What words do we associate with school?'

- Ask oral questions which would anticipate needs in various situations or answer the question of what would happen next, e.g. 'If you were going to bake a cake, what would you need?', 'What would you do if your dog was lost?'

- Ask categorising questions, e.g. 'Name everything you would bring to a picnic'.

- Read questions and ask the child to decide

upon an answer from a given list, e.g. 'Which of these has a tongue but cannot talk?' (man, shoe, radio).

- Use analogies, e.g. robin is to bird as a poodle is to...

- Use numbers, e.g. 2 is to 8 as 3 is to...

- Letters, e.g. 'h' is to 'i' as 'r' is to...

- Materials, e.g. a tyre is to rubber as a window is to...

- Locations, e.g. a typewriter is to an office as a stove is to a...

- Ask the child to pretend to give directions to a stranger on how to get to a particular place in town or describe how to build certain objects.

- Tell a story describing a certain place. The children close their eyes and raise their hands when they think they know the place.

- Ask some 'What would happen if?' questions, e.g. 'What if everyone had three fingers, instead of five?'

- Three or more words are presented to the child. He/she is to name a category that would fit all three.

- Use cartoons or pictures in sequence and ask the child to describe what is happening.

- Ask the children to list vocally all the things they can think of that can carry other things; that have ears, etc.

- Play 'Precise Definitions', e.g. 'Here are some words. Let's tell as much about the word as we can so that everyone will understand what the word means', e.g. 'orange' – citrus fruit, orange in colour, sweet taste, has segments and seeds, rich in vitamin C, etc.

- Play – this can lead on to the game 'Three Little Words'.

- Bird, Beast Or Fish game (other categories can be used). 'Word man' chooses a category and points to a child. That child must give an example of the given category within 10 seconds. No repetitions to be accepted.

- Play 'categories' – the players decide on a category, e.g. animals, places, food. The first player names an animal, for instance. The next player uses the last letter of the word for the first letter of his word and so on.

- Read a sentence to the child. Then ask the child to say the same idea in as many different ways as possible.

- Orally, give the child the name of an occupation and ask him to tell what kind of work is done and what sort of tools the person uses to accomplish his work.

- Avoid extraneous sounds when blending.

To develop auditory synthesis

- Ask the child to count the number of syllables in a word while an adult says it slowly.

- Use kinaesthetic letters (e.g. sandpaper) and ask the child to trace the letters as he sounds them.

- Ask the child to respond to questions such as: 'If b-o-r-n is born, what is t-o-r-n?'

- Ask the child to work out riddles, e.g. 'It is a short 'i' word', 'It begins with 'p'', 'It ends with 'g''.

- Can the children make up their own riddles?

- Ask the child to place his/her finger under each letter as he sounds it and then sweep his/her fingers under the whole word as he/she blends the sounds.

- Plastic/cut-out letters can be pushed together as the child is blending the sounds orally.

- Use phonic exercises. For example,
    1. ask the child to circle the beginning, missing sound: 'The old man was very -oor' (b, p, d);
    2. fill in the blank with a word that starts with the same sound;
    3. ask the child to fill in the missing letter of a rhyme.

- Show the child a whole word. While he/she is looking at it, separate the letters. Take the first letter, say it, and at the same time move it towards the second letter, move them both towards the third, etc., continuing to say the sounds while moving them together.

- Prepare printed lists of words, and record the lists on tapes. The child looks at the words, listens to the tape, and then repeats them onto the tape. Next the adult says each syllable, then the child says the same syllable on the tape where space has been left. Then at the end, the child is asked by the tape to 'say the whole word'.

- Play lotto games.

- Relate syllable learning to music. Ask the children to clap beats to syllables of words in familiar songs.

- Sound out action words to the child which he/she may follow once the instruction is understood, e.g. 'c-l-a-p'.

- Use a word wheel for showing blends and phonograms.

- Play 'New Zoo'. The names of the two familiar animals are blended to make a new word, e.g. turtle and turkey = turkle. The children can then draw their new animal.

- Use letter tiles/scrabble pieces to help blend sounds.

- Encourage imitation of correct grammatical expressions.

- Use visual cues to help initially in eliciting verbal responses.

- Use choral reading.

- Help the child develop the skill of word associations, e.g. man and...(woman).

- Use grammatical exercises, e.g. ask the child to supply the appropriate tense of a given word: 'Yesterday I...',
'Today I...'
'Tomorrow I...'

- Read or tape a story and have the child fill in the suffixes (ing, ment, able, ly) after each appropriate word in the story.

- Give the child a stimulus word and ask him/her to respond with as many different words as he/she can by changing endings. Cards with the endings written on them may be used for visual clues.

- Use well known TV commercials. Give the first few words. The child then completes the commercial with the correct word, e.g. 'Beanz Meanz...', 'For the lady who loves...'

- Give a stimulus word to the child and ask for a word that means the same thing.

- Present sentences where the root word can be changed by adding suffixes to complete the missing word,
e.g. 'Something that is used to freeze foods is called a...', 'Something that is used to grind meat is called a...'

- Ask a question which the child answers by turning it into a statement.

- Show the child a picture of one object: 'This is a...'

- Show a picture of the same object in duplicate: 'These are...'

- Orally present a sentence with an obvious error in structure or meaning, e.g. 'The book sat down and read the magazine'. The children are to identify and correct the error.

- A story containing grammatical errors is read aloud. The child indicates each time he/she hears an error.

- Use scrambled sentences for sequencing.

To increase auditory figure-ground

- Play background music while the child is working independently for set periods of time.

- Help the child select relevant from irrelevant sounds by reducing potentially distracting visual stimuli by having the child cover his/her eyes.

- Use tapes to begin to develop sound selectivity using cue questions before the audio is heard or identifying questions after the audio is heard.

- Ask the child to keep a log of classroom disturbances. Discuss the situations named with the child to increase awareness of the background noise conditions that interfere with his/her learning.

- Give preferential seating to child away from the background noise.

- Move towards the child, making visual contact, when attention is necessary and there is background interference.

- Touch the child to gain attention to focus on a particular direction, activity, etc. when background noise is present.

- Call the child by name before asking a question.

- Provide a study card.

- Provide the child with ear plugs for use when independent work needs to be completed.

The above games could, yet again, be carried out in circle time. As well as training to strengthen a learner's use of the auditory modality, visual strategies may be used for support.

Visual strategies to aid under-standing (semantics and pragmatics)

Our minds are designed naturally to make use of information from our past in order to make sense of the present and anticipate the future so we can then deal with the demands it makes on us.

Communication is part of this process and can be supported by the use of contextual cues. By minimising distractions and emphasising salient cues learners can be helped to understand what is required of them. Speech is a cheap commodity which is overused and transient. It is here in the present but soon gone, whereas visual cues can be more stable over time. As accomplished speakers, educationalists frequently fail to acknowledge the power of visual cues. The classroom and the home each have an implicit etiquette, where activities happen in certain ways at set times in specific places. Learners with speech and communication difficulties may need the following visual cues emphasised as they may not make as much use of them as accomplished communicators like yourself.

Body language
Facial expression;
body orientation and proximity;
posture;
body movement;
reaching, touching and pointing;
eye contact, direction and shifting of gaze.

Natural environmental cues
Furniture arrangement;
location and movement of people and objects;
printed material such as signs, logos, signals, labels and prices, written messages, instructions, post it notes, choices, menus;
directions on packages, machines or businesses.

Traditional tools for organisation and giving information
Calendars, daily planners;
schedules, TV guides, what's on guides;
shopping lists, notes, menus;
signs, labels;
maps;
programmes of study, recipe books;
cheque books, telephone books;
user guides.

Specially designed tools for specific needs

Schedules and mini schedules. These may outline part of the day, all of the day or the week. They may refer to task organisers (see below). They may show what is happening or what is now not going to happen. These may be for all the class to use or for a specific child who may have the schedule by his or her desk or in an organiser.

Personalised calendars. These are extensions of the above to include longer-term and more personalised information.

Choice boards. These show a range of choices including the ones not on offer that might normally be expected. These are indicated by placing a cross on top of them or the international prohibited symbol ø.

Task organisers and cook books. These are step-by-step prompts to help a learner complete a task. The process is like a simple cook book recipe but can be applied to any multiple stage task. Construction kit pictorial guides to making a model are good examples of the technique. These may include individualised worksheets that show what the task is, what materials are required, the stages of the task and how it will be finished. TEACCH suggests using traditional established organising principles to structure tasks, e.g. left to right (in western cultures) and top down.

TEACCH* principles

What is the task?
How much is to be done?
When is it finished?
What to do next?

(Schopler and Mesibov 1985)

(*Treatment and education of autistic and related communication handicapped children)

People and activity locators
These provide information about where the key people in the learner's life are at particular times.

Labels and environmental structure
Public spaces tend to have signs to help those who are unfamiliar with them find their way around and use the facilities available, e.g. exit signs and signs to 'holes in the wall', toilets and telephones. Learners may need to be taught to make use of existing cues but may need the additional support of labelling areas and items. Existing good classroom practice of 'a place' for everything and everything returned to its place can be made more explicit through the use of additional labelled containers and/or marked out areas or boundaries. For example, the carpeted area is a place for listening to stories or reading quietly. Areas of playgrounds may be allocated to different types of play. Tuck shop or dinner queues can be structured using a line of numbered circles.

Photographs
Photographs can be used to provide an explicit guide to an activity or task showing each stage or just the completion. They may be used to show the desired location of the task or an

actual activity. They may show key people. Photographs need to clearly indicate the key element to be considered.

Visual bridges

These are lists or tables of activities undertaken in one setting which are then taken with the learner to another setting to provide a basis for communication, e.g between home and school (Hodgon 1995).

Overlay keyboards for computers and on-screen grids

Software on computers such as Concept and Clicker can provide visual and spoken prompts for writing and learning activities. Grids can contain words, pictures and symbols from a variety of symbol sets.

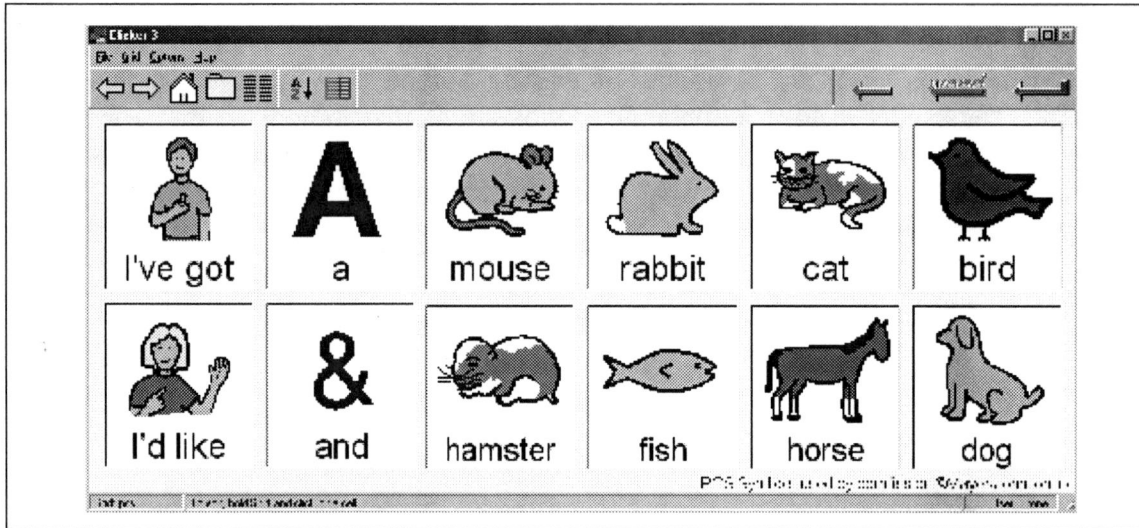

Figure 7. A clicker grid using Mayer Johnson Symbols for writing on a computer. Illustration courtesy of Crick Software.

Figure 8. A point grid using Rebus Symbols for writing on a computer. Illustration courtesy of Advisory Unit. Note: some symbols used may be more abstract than others. In designing a visual support such as a schedule, the user's level of communicational ability will need to be taken into account. The following levels of communication described by the TEACCH programme may be useful.

TEACCH levels of communication
1. Motoric level, where the child uses or leads the adult to a desired object or place.
2. Object level, where the child gives an adult an object to signify an activity.
3. Picture level, where the child gives an adult a picture/photo of an activity.
4. Written level, where the child gives a written word or a symbol to an adult or writes a word for the activity.
5. Augmentative aid: the use of a communication board or aid such as a filofax of symbols, an overlay keyboard or a communication aid.
6. Speech.   (Schopler and Mesibov 1985)

Picture or object exchange systems

This begins with teaching a non-verbal student to exchange a picture or object referring to a desired item with a teacher, who immediately responds to the request. Verbal prompts are not used, thus building immediate initiation and avoiding prompt dependency. The system goes on to teach discrimination of symbols and then puts them all together in simple 'sentences'. Children are also taught to comment and answer direct questions. Many pre-schoolers using PECS also begin developing speech. The system has been used with adolescents and adults who have a wide array of communicative, cognitive and physical difficulties (Bondy and Frost 1994).

Visual strategies: Institutional self review

visual aids

- Is the visual aid important for the learner's understanding?
- Is the use of the visual support modelled by an adult?
- Is the visual aid unambiguous and concrete?
- Does the visual aid match the cognitive level of the child (see above)?
- Can the skills supported by the visual aid be practised and applied in other settings?

Questioning strategies

Strategy 9:

Reading/language demand

This has been changed to language demand so that we can encompass both auditory and print versions of language.

Is the reading demanded from the tasks appropriate? Is the readability level too difficult? Is the page layout of materials cluttered or too busy? Do key words need to be taught?

There are more questions than answers
Johnny Nash (1974) CBS records

The current move to more directed teaching, where 'how you teach it' is prescribed as well as 'what you teach', has increased pressure on teachers to adopt whole-class teaching methods in order to meet the literacy and numeracy targets. A re-emphasis on and extension of 'traditional' question and answer sessions is still open to 'traditional' criticisms. Back in the seventies Westbury (1972) suggested four responsibilities of teachers:

1. task attention (keeping learners on task);

2. control;

3. coverage of content;

4. practice for mastery.

Westbury believed that question and answer sessions helped teachers to carry out these responsibilities with minimum effort but was critical that they led to nominal mastery of the content without the learners fully understanding or utilising new knowledge.

The two-thirds rule may become valid again. 'Two thirds of every lesson is made up of talk and two thirds of the talk comes from the teacher' (Flanders 1963). This does not give much room for communication or language development. It turns education into the transfer of knowledge from teacher to pupil with little opportunity for engagement or negotiation. 'Much of the knowledge which is presented to children in schools requires them to accommodate views of the world which differ from their everyday understanding' (Barnes 1975).

The Code of Practice has been suggested as a progressive focusing on the needs of the child starting from the premise that the school should assume a diversity of learning needs amongst its pupils and differentiate the curriculum to take this into account. The views and understanding of the child need to be taken into account as part of the dynamic planning and action of the IEP. This is expressed by Barnes (1975): 'Once one adopts an interaction view of education, it becomes as valid to see educational failure as the school's failure to understand a child's messages, as to see it as the child's failure to understand the school's messages'. Bernstein (1970) observed: 'If the

96

culture of the teacher is to become part of the consciousness of the child, then the culture of the child must be in consciousness of the teacher'. This can be achieved by taking into account the monitoring that different participants within the IEP are able to carry out.

The following levels of questioning may help a teacher or adult to review the form of questioning they use in their teaching.

Questioning levels

Level 1

The information is supplied directly in front of the child, or has just been removed. The response is a short (one word) answer, or non-verbal:
- find one like this
- what did you hear/touch/see?
- what's this?
- show me what you heard.

Level 2

The information is supplied but isn't directly apparent. The child has to select *what* to attend to, e.g. size, colour, function of object, etc.:
- find one that can cut
- what is happening in this scene?
- what colour is this?
- find one that is...and goes...
- who? what? where?
- how are these different?
- name something that is a...

Level 3

The language doesn't relate directly to what they see/hear, but instead the child must think and re-order the information given:
- what will happen next?
- what could he say?
- tell the story
- do this, then this
- how are these the same?
- what is a...?
- find the things that are not...
- name something that can...but is not a...
- tell me how...

Level 4

The child has to reason beyond what is said, heard or seen. The child needs to draw on past experience, make parallels and examine causes and effects, as well as justify the decision made:
- what will happen if...?
- why will...?
- what made it happen?
- what could you do?

- why wouldn't it...?
- why would it...?
- why is this called a...?
- what could we use?
- how can we tell?

(source: Caroline Emby SLT)

Word finding difficulties

Strategies which may help include the following.

- Allow the child time to respond.
  Encourage the child to ask himself/herself.
  What does it look like?
  What do you do with it?
  What sound does it begin with?
  How many syllables has it?
  What does it sound like?
  Where would you find it?
  Can you show it with your hands?

- Provide visual prompts using an object/symbol/sign or picture.

- Use gesture for it.

- Provide an associated word.

- A descriptive clue: 'It is cold, white and you lick it...'.

- A phonic clue, e.g. 'It begins with an I'.

- A definition: 'It is made of cream that is really cold...'.

Strategy 10:

Attention (given or expected)

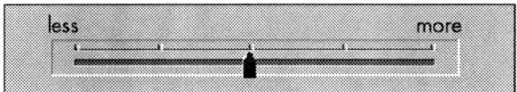

The importance of the development of attention in the context of language has been stressed above.

  Decreasing the amount of noise and increasing the degree of visual clarity and structure of activities and routines as described above will help a child to attend to the important elements of a task.

Using Information and Communications Technology

The following SCAA guidance will be of use to the ICT coordinator working with colleagues to harness ICT opportunities for language development. The classic framework of Joan Tough describing language usage for learning may be of use in assessing language opportunities in ICT to develop the speaking and listening skills outlined in the programmes of study at Key Stages 1 and 2.

Speaking and listening

Explore, develop and clarify ideas, predicting outcomes, and discussing possibilities; describe events, observations and experiences, explaining choices and giving reasons.

Develop and explain ideas, predicting, sharing opinions and reporting events, make exploratory and tentative comments when ideas are being collected together, and make reasoned, evaluative comments as discussion moves to conclusions or action.

(SCAA 1996)

Clearly, these are ambitious but appropriate long-term goals for learners with language and communication difficulties. These need to be prioritised and structured for individual learners.

1. REVIEW
What do you do already?

- Do you know what opportunities for language work exist in ICT?
- Are you aware how language skills can improve ICT?

2. PLAN
Could you plan for a greater emphasis on language skills?

- Include language developments in the policy statements /plan for IT in the school.
- Highlight language opportunities in all ICT schemes of work.
- Prepare some ICT vocabulary lists for each Key Stage.
- Improve the range of reading and listening resources (e.g. books, newspapers, tapes poems) available for IT work.
- Consider progression in language development within a unit of work, a year, a Key Stage.

3. IDENTIFY
What else might be going on in your school?

- Who else can you speak to about language development (e.g. other subject coordinators, language support staff, head teacher)?
- Is there a policy for language development in your school?
- Can you obtain advice/help from LEA advisors/consultants/web sites?
- Are there further resources or material the school might consider acquiring?

4. EVALUATE
How successful are you?

- Are skills in speaking and listening, and writing and reading, helping children to improve their understanding and knowledge of ICT?
- How specifically is work in ICT helping children to become more competent in their use of language?

Information handling
Abstract numerical information can be presented in a visually concrete manner using computer created charts.

Communication of ideas
Multimedia software can present interactive displays to illustrate concepts. Pictures and speech can be combined in illustrations and to provide support for a range of learning tasks – see p.101.

A discussion of the selection and use of communication aids is beyond the scope of this book but there are a number of software programs and devices available. See the section on communication aids in 'Resources'.

Modelling
Interactive talking stories can provide stimuli for shared discussion as described above, e.g. 'What happened when you clicked on that?', 'What shall we do next?', 'That was scary!'

Control
Computers and simple programmable toys/robots can provide opportunities for talk about directions and sequences.

See the list of software suppliers at the end of this book.

Postscript

This book has sought to address the following questions.
- How can there be agreement on the targets when the pupil functions differently in different contexts?
- Should the aim for pupils be to access the curriculum or social communication?
- How can speech and language targets be met across a range of subject areas?
- Given that language is dynamic, can the static IEP document provide a feasible blueprint for action?
- Can the challenge of monitoring IEPs for speech and language targets be realistically met?
- To what extent can teachers deliver specialist strategies to meet IEP targets in the absence of speech therapy support?
- How can new developments in ICT support IEP delivery for students with speech and language difficulties?

The different sections of this book have attempted to provide a framework for individual schools to audit their current practice and develop appropriate responses. The approaches we have suggested may involve more work than 'off-the-shelf' quick fixes but we consider the adoption of a whole-school and holistic approach to language and communication to be central to effective learning for all children.

Resources

Social skills training

Anderson-Wood, L. and Roe Smith, B. (1994) *Working with Pragmatics*. Bicester: Winslow.

Johnson, M. (1992) *Functional Language in the Classroom*. Manchester: Metropolitan University.

Kelly, A. (1996) *Talkabout: A Social Communication Skills Package*. Bicester: Winslow.

Leicestershire County Council Education Department (1998) *Autism: How to Help Your Young Child*. London NAS.

Rinaldi, W. (1992) *Social Use of Language Programme*. Windsor: NFER-Nelson.

Circle time

Ashford Learning Support Service Team, Kent County Council, *Circle Time Inset Pack*. Ashford Learning Resource Centre.

Bliss, T. and Robinson, G. (1995) *Developing Circle Time*. Lucky Duck Publications.

Curry, M. and Broomfield, C. (1994) *Personal and Social Education for Primary Schools through Circle Time*. NASEN Enterprises.

Goldthorpe, M. (1998) *Effective IEPs through Circle Time*. Wisbech LDA.

McNamara, S. and Moreton, G. (1995) *Changing Behaviour: Teaching Children with Emotional and Behavioural Difficulties in Primary and Secondary Classrooms*. London: David Fulton Publishers.

Mosley, J. (1993) *Turn Your School Around*. Wisbech: LDA.

Mosley, J. (1996) *Quality Circle Time in the Primary School*. Wisbech: LDA.

Video: *Coming Round to Circle Time*. Bristol: Lucky Duck Publications.

Social stories

Attwood, T. (1998) *Asperger's Syndrome: A Guide for Parents and Professionals*. London: Jessica Kingsley Publishers.

Gray, Carol (ed.) (1994) *The New Social Story Book*. Arlington: Future Horizons (available from Winslow in the UK).

Gray, Carol (1994) *Comic Strip Conversations*. Arlington: Future Horizons (available from Winslow in the UK).

Myles-Smith, B. and Simpson, R. L. (1998) *Asperger Syndrome: A Guide for Educators and Parents*. Austin, Texas: Pro-Ed.

Visual strategies

Hodgon, L. (1995) *Visual Strategies for Improving Communication*. Michigan: Quirk Roberts (available from Winslow in the UK).

Circles of friends

Newton, C., Taylor, G. and Wilson, D. (1996) 'Circles of friends: an inclusive approach to meeting emotional and behavioural needs', *Educational Psychology in Practice* **11**(4).

Peerpoint, J., Forest, M. and Snow, J. (1992) *The Inclusion Papers*. Toronto: Inclusion Press.

Taylor, G. (1977) 'Community building in schools: developing a circle of friends', *Educational and Child Psychology* **14**(3).

Whitaker, P., Barratt, P., Joy, H., Potter, M. and Thomas, G. (1998) 'Children with autism and peer group support: using "circles of friends"', *BJSE* **25**(2).

Software suppliers

Crick Computing
1 The Avenue
Spinney Hill
Northampton NN3 6BA
Tel. 01604 671691
http://www.cricksoft.com
(suppliers of Mayer Johnson Symbol sets)

Advisory Unit
126 Great North Road
Hatfield
Hertfordshire AL9 5JZ
Tel. 01707 266714
http://www.advisory-unit.org.uk/
(suppliers of software for overlay keyboards and switch access)

Widgit Software
102 Radford Road
Leamington Spa CV31 1LF
Tel. 01926 885303
http://www.widgit.com/index.htm
(suppliers of a variety of symbol sets including Rebus)

Inclusive Technology Ltd
Saddleworth Business Centre
Huddersfield Road
Delph
Oldham Ol3 5DF
http://www.inclusive.co.uk/
infosite/ithome.htm

Communication aids and access devices

Advisory Centre for Education (ACE)
Ormerod School
Waynflete Road
Headington
Oxford OX3 8DD
Tel. 01865 763508
http://www.rmplc.co.uk/orgs/acecent/homepage.html
(centre supplying advice and software for access and communication)

References

Adams, J. I. (1997) *Autism PDD More Creative Ideas*. Ontario: Adams Publications (available from Winslow in the UK).

Attwood, A. (1998) *Asperger Syndrome: A Guide for Educators and Parents*. London: Jessica Kingsley Publishers.

Barnes, D. (1975) *From Communication to Curriculum*. London: Penguin.

Baron-Cohen, S. (1996) *Mindblindness: An Essay on Autism and Theory of Mind*. Cambridge, Massachusetts: MIT Press.

Bernstein, B. (1970) 'Education cannot compensate for society', *New Society* 26 February.

Bieber, J. (producer) (1994) 'Learning difficulties and social skills with Richard LaVoie: last one picked...first one picked on', Washington, DC: Public Broadcasting Service.

Bloom, L. and Lacey, M. (1998) *Language Development and Language Disorders*. London: Wiley.

Bondy, A. and Frost, L. (1994) 'Educational approaches in preschool: behaviour techniques in a public school setting', in Schopler, E. and Mesibov, G. (eds) *Learning and Cognition in Autism*. New York: Plenum Press.

Cazan, L., Dennisin, C. and Coleman, J. (1996) *Getting Through: Effective Communication in the Teenage Years*. London: The BT Forum

DfE (1994) *Code of Practice on the Identification and Assessment of Special Educational Needs*. London: HMSO (EDUC JO22465NJ 5/94).

DfEE (1997a) *Excellence for All Children: Meeting Special Educational Needs*. London. HMSO.

DfEE (1997b) *Improving Literacy in Primary Schools*: www.open.gov.uk./dfee/seu/literacy/index.htm

DfEE (1997c) *The SENCO Guide*. London: HMSO.

Evans, R., Docking, J. and Evans, C. (1996) 'Improving support for children with special educational needs', *Support for Learning* 11, 99–104.

Emby, C. (1998) Course materials on autism course, Canterbury Christ Church College.

Feuerstein, R. (1976) 'Mediated learning experience: a theoretical basis for human modifiability during adolescence', in Mittler, P. (ed.) *Research and Practice in Mental Retardation*, **Vol. II**, Baltimore, Maryland: University Park Press.

Flanders, N. E. (1963) 'Intent, action and feedback: a preparation for teaching', in Amidon, J. E. J. and Hough, J. B. (eds) (1967) *Interaction Analysis: Theory, Research and Application*. New York: Holt, Rhinehart and Wilson.

Grandin, T. (1995) *Thinking in Pictures*. New York: Doubleday.

Gray, C. A. (1997) 'Teaching children with autism to read social situations', in Quill, K. A. (ed.) (1997) *Teaching Children with Autism: Strategies to Enhance Communication and Socialisation*. London: Delmar Publishers.

Halliday, M. A. K. (1975) *Learning How to Mean – Explorations in the Development of Language*. London: Edward Arnold.

Hart, S. (1988) 'Paperwork or practice? Shifting the emphasis of the Code towards teaching, learning and inclusion', *Support for Learning* 13(2), 2 May, p.76.

103

Hundert, J. (1995) *Enhancing Social Competence in Young Students: School Based Approaches*. Austin, Texas: Pro-Ed.

Jordan, R. and Powell, S. (1996) *Understanding and Teaching Children with Autism*. London: Wiley.

Lloyd, S. R. and Berthelot, C. (1992) *Self-empowerment: How to Get What You Want from Life*. London: Kogan Page.

Locke, A. (1985) *Teaching Talking*. London: NFER-Nelson.

Martin, D. and Miller, C. (1996) *Speech and Language Difficulties in the Classroom*. London: David Fulton Publishers.

McTear, M. F. and Conti-Ramsden, G. (1992) *Pragmatic Disability in Children: Studies in Disorders of Communication*. London: Whurr Publications.

Mead, G. H. (1934) *Mind, Self and Society*. Chicago, Illinois: University of Chicago Press.

Moorcroft, G. (1998) Course materials presented on autism course, Canterbury Christ Church College.

OFSTED (1996) *The Implementation of the Code of Practice for Pupils with Special Educational Needs*. London: HMSO.

OFSTED (1997) *The SEN Code of Practice: Two Years On*. London: HMSO.

Peeters, T. (1997) *Autism: From Theoretical Understanding to Educational Intervention*. London: Whurr Publications.

Pinker, S. (1994) *The Language Instinct*. London: Penguin.

Pearcey, N. (1996) 'Circles within circles', in Mosley, J. (1996) *Quality Circle Time in the Primary School*. Wisbech: LDA.

Quill, K. A. (ed.) (1997) *Teaching Children with Autism: Strategies to Enhance Communication and Socialisation*. London: Delmar Publishers.

Rappaport, M. (1996) 'Strategies for promoting language acquisition in children with autism', in Maurice, C. (ed.) *Behavioral Interventions for Young Children with Autism*. Austin, Texas: Pro-Ed.

Reynell, J. (1977) *Reynell Developmental Language Scales (revised)*. Windsor: NFER.

SCAA (1995) *Planning the Curriculum*. Hayes: SCAA.

SCAA (1996) *Information Technology and the Use of Language*, ref: Com/96/645. Hayes: SCAA.

SCAA (1997) *Use of Language: A Common Approach*, ref: Com/97/640. Hayes: SCAA.

Schopler, E. and Mesibov, G. (eds) (1985) *Communication Problems in Autism*. New York: Plenum Press.

Spence, S. (1977) *Social Skills Training with Children and Adolescents*. Windsor: NFER-Nelson.

Taylor, G. (1997) 'Community building in schools: developing a circle of friends', *Educational and Child Psychology* **14**(3).

Tizard, B. and Hughes, M. (1984) *Young Children Learning, Talking and Thinking at Home and School*. London: Fontana.

Tough, J. (1977) *The Development of Meaning*. London: Unwin Education Books.

TTA (1998) *National Standards for Special Educational Needs Co-ordinators*. London: TTA.

Webster, A. and Webster, C. (1995) *Profiles of Development: Planning for Individual Progress within the National Curriculum*. Bristol: Avec Designs.

Wells, G. (1985) *Language, Learning and Education*. Windsor: NFER-Nelson.

Westbury, I. (1972) 'Conventional classrooms, open classrooms and the technology of teaching', *Journal of Curriculum Studies* **5**(2).

Williams, D. (1996) *Autism: An Inside-out Approach*. London: Jessica Kingsley Publishers.

Printed in the United Kingdom by
Lightning Source UK Ltd., Milton Keynes
139843UK00001B/6/A